THE
CHRISTIAN
WORKING
WOMAN

THE CHRISTIAN WORKING WOMAN

MARY WHELCHEL

Fleming H. Revell Company
Old Tappan, New Jersey

Library of Congress Cataloging-in-Publication Data

Whelchel, Mary.
  The Christian working woman.

  1. Women—Conduct of life.   2. Women—Employment.
3. Whelchel, Mary.   I. Title.
BJ1610.W52   1986   248.8'43   85-23835
ISBN 0-8007-1477-6

To my mother

My role model for Christian womanhood,
whose walk with God continually challenges me,
whose friendship constantly encourages me,
whose prayers faithfully support me,
and whose love quietly affirms me

Contents

Preface

~

Most people who write books relate that they have had deep, life-long desires to be a writer. Not so with me. I have written this book for one reason: to encourage and challenge Christian women who, for whatever reason, are a part of the working world outside their homes. I am one of those women, and have been for almost fifteen years. So, I write as an insider—one who has made about every mistake you can imagine, and who still struggles with many issues. You will learn about me and my struggles in this role as a working woman as you read through these chapters.

And undoubtedly you will detect what God and I already know—that I don't have all the answers and that God is not finished with me yet. Thankfully, God does not require perfection of us as a prerequisite to service. We don't have to have all our act together in order to be of use to Him. He chooses to use us while we're right in the middle of learning and growing and putting the pieces together. Only a truly powerful and magnificent God could pull that off!

I've discovered that frequently there is little support or encouragement for working women in many Christian environments. In fact, many Christian working women feel quite guilty for entering the working world, even when they have no other option. In the past few years I've made some small attempts to try to remedy that problem, through a small Bible study in my home for women who work, by starting a ministry for working women in my church, and through a radio program called "The Christian Working Woman," which is a fairly new, growing ministry.

I hope this book will continue that gap-filling purpose. I pray that tucked in among these many words, there are some insights that will give direction and hope to Christian working women. I am totally convinced that God's Word is relevant to every issue we face, regardless of our circumstances.

But knowing how to apply biblical principles is not always clear to us. As I've faced various situations, and talked with other women about their particular problems, I've searched for "handles" to put on the Truth of God. I need simple, practical ideas and approaches that help me take the words off the pages of the Bible and make them reality in my everyday life.

This book is a compilation of some of those "ideas" that God has given to me to help me apply His principles to my life as a working woman. I believe the topics discussed are ones that most working women face at one point or another. I have tried to write openly and candidly, as though I were speaking to you directly. I would like to think that by the time you finish reading this, we will be good friends. Mostly, I hope something I've written will help you.

Introduction

≈

Full-Time Job-
Part-Time Christian?

L et me ask you a two-part question: "Why do you
work, and why do you have the particular job you
have?" Do you view your job as simply a means of putting
bread on your table so you can do what you want with the
rest of your time? Do you work just because you have to
earn a living?

Perhaps you would say that you work because you really
enjoy the challenge and you have career ambitions that interest you. Or, maybe you're working to supplement the
family income or to pay for a college education for your
child. Maybe you work just to get out of the house. There
would be, I'm sure, quite a variety of answers to this
question.

My own answers to this question have changed greatly in
the last few years. I entered the working world out of necessity. Becoming a business woman had never been on my list
of aspirations during college or those formative years.
My pursuit of a career was prompted by the necessity of

earning a living for my daughter and myself. I certainly got caught up in advancing my career, and I frequently enjoyed the challenge and rewards of my work. But essentially I was working because I had to. Only in the last few years have I begun to see my job as having any eternal significance.

What I discovered about myself—and what I find true about many Christians in the working world—is that we tend to mentally divide our lives into two parts. Our jobs and the other mundane activities of our lives we tend to classify as "secular," and there is another compartment in our lives that we consider "sacred," which includes our church activities and whatever other ministries we may have. And because our jobs demand so much of our time, the secular department is considerably larger than the sacred department. These designations are not usually conscious ones, but nonetheless they exist in our thinking.

Furthermore, we tend to view ourselves as working people out in the everyday business world in a different light than those who choose a public ministry for their life's work. There is an underlying attitude that those people in public ministries are of more service to God than those of us who are in the working world. We use the term "in full-time Christian service" for people who choose public ministries in a church or Christian organization. Somehow we tend to think that the organization from which we get our paycheck determines whether we're in "full-time Christian service" or not.

Men and women in public ministries are expected to talk about the Lord, to witness, to encourage people, to study God's Word, to pray a lot. But here you and I are, working at secular jobs, and our duties don't exactly lend themselves to talking about the Lord or concentrating on spiritual matters. We have to be concerned with pleasing our bosses, getting the letters typed, answering the telephone, talking with clients, taking orders, teaching our students, attending patients, tracking statistics—whatever particular duties our job encompasses. In our minds we fail to see any connection between these secular duties and our Christian commitment.

Well, is there any connection? A couple of years ago I spoke to the business association at the Christian college my daughter attends, and one of the things I emphasized with this group of Christian young adults getting ready to embark on careers in business was this: *If you have committed your life to Jesus Christ, you are in "full-time Christian service."* God expects as much of you as He expects of preachers and missionaries. There are no "sacred" and "secular" departments with God. The same power available to people in public ministries is available to those of us who go to our working worlds every day.

The sooner we can understand that God sees us as total beings, the sooner we'll be able to view our jobs as He would have us view them. He is interested in every part of our lives. He has a special plan for each of us, and no one person's life plan is any more important than another's in His view. He is no respecter of persons.

If you are sure of God's direction into the working world for you, it is just as sacred, just as important to God, and of just as much service to Him as anything else you could do. It is not "second best"; it is not the alternative for those who have never sensed a call into a public ministry. It is full-time Christian service!

Do you view your job as *the* place where God has you at

this time for His purposes, to teach you and to use you as a light in darkness?

You may say, "Well, I've never thought about it that way. I went to college, or I graduated from high school, and then I had to work, so I found the best job I could, and I'm working! I don't know if I've ever really considered whether this is where God wants me to be or not."

Do you think it's less important for those of us who work in the business world to know that we're where God wants us to be than it is for our ministers or missionaries? When we get up to go to work in the morning, we should have a sense of commitment to what God has called us to do, and a surety that we are headed to the place where He wants us to be, just as much as our pastors do when they go to their offices at our churches.

As I mentioned earlier, it wasn't too long ago that I thought of my job as a separate part of my life. At that point I was placing too much importance on advancing my career, and I did not view my job as God's mission for me. But now I realize that God is not inefficient. He would not have me spend such a great part of my life doing something that is not important to Him. Indeed, He intends for me, and for all Christians in the working world, to see our job as His mission field for our service to Him.

In John 17 Jesus prays for His disciples and says:

> *I am no more in the world; and yet they themselves are in the world, and I come to Thee. Holy Father, keep them in Thy name. . . . I do not ask Thee to take them out of the world, but to keep them from the evil one. They are not of the world, even as I am not of the world. . . . As Thou didst send Me*

into the world, I also have sent them into the world (11, 15, 16, 18).

Jesus said He was praying this not only for His disciples then, but for all of us who would believe in Him. That's you and me!

You know, God could have taken us to Him as soon as we accepted Christ. Why not? That would have been nice for us. We would be relieved of all this grief and sin and work and sorrow—and just be immediately transported to His presence.

Or He could supply every need we have so that we could all live together in separate Christian communities, and not have to associate with all the evil that characterizes the world today. But He has so arranged it that we *have* to be in the world—we have to go out and make our living in this world.

Have you ever thought of this: God has designed work as the common denominator for the Christian and non-Christian, and the job is the place where the Christian must meet the non-Christian world. This is no accident. God has planned it this way.

Likely you have heard sermons that touched on this subject already. But I just wonder if, like me, you have been treating your job simply as a necessary part of your life— something to be endured, hopefully financially rewarding, maybe even interesting. But you never really look at it as your mission in life.

Jesus said He has sent us into the world. None of us is exempted from this. Regardless of your personality or your talents or your abilities, if you are a Christian, you are *sent*.

It's not a matter of waiting for a "call." It's not a matter of deciding whether we want to be sent or not. Christ has sent us into the world—there are no options.

And where is your world into which you are sent? It includes your working world, whether that world is an office or a store or a classroom or a hospital or a factory. That is the world into which you are sent.

Is it really any mystery why God would have His people out in this working world? After all, that's where the people are who need Him. God can, and indeed does, purposely send us out into the working world as His witnesses, His light. Is this any less important or of lesser value to God than someone who is in Africa translating Scripture? No.

In answer to the question I posed at the beginning, Why do you work, and why do you have the particular job you have? can we not then answer that our jobs are the part of the world into which God has sent us to minister. That job is your corner of the world where you are sent. If you don't cover it, nobody else will.

Okay, you may say, so God has sent us. So, our corner of the world is just as important as any other corner. But when I get to my corner, I can't preach or teach or witness all day. I have to work. How can that be a mission?

Well, you see, the neat thing about being sent into the working world is that we get in on equal footing. We're not a different set—a minority—we're one of the gang. Our ministers can't get in there, as ministers, and get to know the people we work with as we do. They would be outsiders. But we're there. We have a right to be there. We have a duty to be there.

And in that place where we are sent, though we cannot

preach or teach or continually witness, our lives can become the inescapable witness to what God can do for and with any person who is committed to Him. Our fellow workers cannot ignore or deny a witness that is lived in front of their eyes.

In Matthew 5:16 we read that Jesus said:

> *Let your light so shine before men, that they may see your good works, and glorify your Father which is in heaven* (KJV).

How can we be lights and witnesses in the part of the world to which we are sent? First Peter 3:15 tells us to always be ready to give an answer to everyone who asks us to give an account for the hope that is in us, yet with gentleness and reverence.

Let me assure you of this: If you begin to view your job as the place in the world where God has sent you—and only you—to be His witness and His light, it won't be long before you will have an opportunity to give an account for the hope that is in you. The most effective witness is one that comes as a result of a question. And if you relate to your job as your mission from God, your behavior and your life will be different. That difference will cause people to be thirsty, and sooner or later they'll ask you, in one way or another, why you are different.

But it begins with a changed attitude toward our jobs. We cannot treat our jobs as separate parts of our lives—secular rather than sacred. They must be viewed as the corner of the world into which we have been sent by Jesus.

As one who is still learning this lesson herself, I want to encourage you to ask God to change your thinking about your job. It will give it a completely new importance. You'll be amazed at how much more meaningful everyday life becomes when you view your job as your mission, as indeed it is.

In the chapters that follow, we'll first take a look at ourselves, our attitudes and attributes, and how we can prepare ourselves for covering that corner of the world to which we have been sent. Then we'll discuss some problem situations and how to use God's principles in dealing with them. We'll see that, truly, God's Word is relevant to every issue we face.

Chapter One

Multiple Roles, But One Identity

Whether a woman is working to supplement the family income, to fulfill lifelong aspirations, or from necessity as a single woman or single parent, she usually finds herself playing several roles. Although multiple roles are not new, the working woman of today seems to be struggling for identity. Which of her roles is most important? In which role does she find her real self?

Feeling herself pressured by her own expectations, as well as those of her family, employers, and friends, she falls prey to the "Superwoman Complex." She senses an unspoken demand from society to give a "walk on water" performance at all times. Trying to be all things to all people, she becomes a prime candidate for an identity crisis.

How well I remember the shock to my own identity when I began my career. I was selected as one of the first female sales representatives for one of America's leading companies. And I was immersed into a very male world, almost overnight—the only female rep in my office, and the first female sales rep most of my customers had ever seen. In addition I was struggling with singleness, having recently been divorced. Since I had never planned to be a career woman, and certainly never a divorced woman, these were unfamiliar roles that were thrust upon me unexpectedly.

At the time I probably would not have verbalized my situation as an identity crisis, but indeed those new circumstances were the beginning of a long struggle for my identity. I wanted to be a very female female, not losing whatever softness and femininity I possessed. I wanted a special man to validate that femininity. And I wanted to be a supersuccessful career woman. My daughter was eight at the time, so in addition I certainly wanted to be a first-rate mother. I was a Christian, too, and tried to fit my Christianity into all these other roles and demands. How could I possibly make all the roles come together successfully in one very human and very fallible person—me?

What began to happen was that the roles became very unbalanced. I was so anxious and determined to succeed in my career, and so desperate to be affirmed as a woman as well, that my whole emphasis in life shifted to those goals and objectives. Those roles took priority and the others suffered. In particular, my relationship with God really took a backseat. Though I was a Christian, I lost that unique quality that every Christian should have—that of light and salt in a dark and tasteless world. I blended in with everyone else. I did not want to be different. I wanted to be a sophisticated, savvy business lady, and I wanted to attract a male counterpart. That was the focus of my life for many years.

Though my circumstances precipitated my role-juggling identity imbalance, I cannot use my career or my divorce as an excuse for my failure to have balanced priorities. It is certainly possible for Christians with varied duties and roles to have a balanced, Christ-honoring perspective of their roles and to perform well in each without having misplaced priorities. So, the many "hats" I wore were not the problem.

I now know it was my "evil, unbelieving heart" (Hebrews 3:12) that caused the identity crisis I was experiencing. It was my own lack of understanding of who God is and how He feels about me, and what His intentions are toward me. And because my comprehension of God was inaccurate and inadequate, I was afraid to trust Him. Isn't it true that we often try to blame our roles or our circumstances for problems that really begin with our refusal or inability to believe God and trust Him?

The Fear of Trusting God

That's a common problem, I think—the fear of really trusting God with everything in our lives. My particular fear was that God would demand I give up my goals of a successful career and a marriage with "Mr. Right," and substitute in their place some dreadful life of loneliness and drudgery. So, I took over the management of my life, with all the various roles that were expected of me. And in short order, I had my identity pretty well confused. During this period, I kept changing hats between roles, as the occasion demanded. Sometimes I wore the "Mother Hat," sometimes the "Business Hat"; then I would switch to the "Female Hat" and the "Christian Hat" when appropriate. But the roles did not blend, and the transition between hats was neither healthy nor smooth.

Life-Style Rationalization

I was frequently a different person under the different hats. That role juggling fostered hypocrisy in many areas, and led to life-style rationalizations on my part. You know what life-style rationalization is, don't you? It is when you convince yourself that what you are doing is necessary for success or happiness—whatever drive or desire is upper-most at the time—and therefore your actions are justifiable. It's very similar to situation ethics, which has been prevalent for quite a few years. I rationalized that certain social practices were necessary in the high-powered sales business I was in, and though incompatible with my "Christian Hat," they were necessary when wearing my "Business Hat." When I wore my "Female Hat," I rationalized behavior that would have been totally unacceptable with my "Mother Hat" or my "Christian Hat."

Life-style rationalization is not unusual when we're juggling roles and confused as to our real identity. You can spot a great deal of it these days among Christians. My own identity crisis had led me to an unacceptable and sinful life-style rationalization.

A Turning Point

There came a turning point in my life where I saw the futility of this role juggling, and I found the hat switching was more than I could handle. The best description of the turmoil inside me then is that I was like an emotional yo-yo!

The ups and downs became more and more extreme, and the downs began to last longer than the ups. The guilt of my life-style rationalization and the failure to achieve my self-centered goals and objectives for each of my roles gradually took their toll. This ten-year struggle caused me to begin to become unglued.

My brightest hopes of being a superwoman were crushed. My job suffered, my role as a mother suffered, my relationships suffered, my self-image suffered. I was no longer performing well in any of my roles, I was confused, and I was desperate. It was this desperation that finally brought me to that crucial turning point.

What actually changed at that time was my mind-set. I was so desperate for peace and contentment, that *they* became my goals and objectives. And where could I turn for peace? Obviously, running my own life was not the answer. I had tried that for ten years and failed miserably. So, at the end of my rope, I said to God, "I'm willing to do anything and be anything, if You will only give me peace."

For the first time in many years I truly wanted to be in a right relationship with God more than anything else. This was, finally, the identity that took priority over everything else for me. What a very dumb lady I was to struggle for such a long time, and to wait until I was almost without hope before turning to God for the answer. How I do appreciate His long-suffering and patience with me. I continue to marvel at how He could have put up with me for that long a time. But the story of the prodigal son's return tells us that we have just such a heavenly Father, who gladly receives us back even when we've wasted years and resources and opportunities.

Now that I see the miraculous changes that He has

brought to my life, I ask myself why I did not trust Him sooner. And the answer that comes back is that I did not really understand who God is, and therefore how trustworthy He is. I had been taught the basics of Christianity from my earliest days, had graduated from a Christian college, and was active in church all my life. The fault does not lie with my teaching but rather with my dullness of understanding and the satanic fear of trusting God that was controlling my life. This long identity struggle was the result of my refusal to trust God with my life's direction.

Life-Changing Principles

I believe the principles and truths that changed my life at that turning point and gave me the key to finding my true identity are basic and helpful for anyone who is still struggling with an identity problem. They work for anyone who is changing hats, shifting identities, trying to be what they think they should be or what they think they want to be, and never finding their true identity.

These three basic principles that began to go from my head to my heart are simple beyond belief. Undoubtedly, most of you will nod your head in agreement as you read them. They are not new. Many, many people far more eloquent have stated them much better than I can. Saints through the ages have proclaimed their truth.

Is it really any surprise that the solution to our identity struggles is not found in new philosophies, new psychological theories, or new therapeutic treatments? We think we've come up with a new disorder, peculiar to our high-tech, high-stress, high-powered generation—and we call it an "identity crisis." But our new disorder is just an old problem called "carnality" or "self-centeredness" or "walking after the flesh and not after the Spirit." We try to put a new name on it, give it some respectability thereby, and find new cures for it. But anything short of God's principles and God's solution is a very short-term, unsatisfying answer.

I believe with all my heart that if you will truly believe these three simple principles and implement them in your everyday life, you will put an end to your identity struggle, your life will change, and those fears of trusting God will be no more.

Understanding Who God Is

First I had to really begin to understand who this God is that I claimed to serve and worship.

Isaiah 44:6, 8 tells us our *God is the only God:*

> *Thus says the Lord, the King of Israel and his Redeemer, the Lord of hosts: "I am the first and I am the last, And there is no God besides Me.... Is there any God besides Me, Or is there any other Rock? I know of none."*

In Isaiah 44:24 we see that He is *God the Creator:*

> *Thus says the Lord, your Redeemer, and the one who formed you from the womb, "I, the Lord, am the maker of all things, Stretching out the heavens by Myself, And spreading out the earth all alone."*

Our *God is all-powerful* and does what He pleases:

> *I know that the Lord is great, And that our Lord is above all gods. Whatever the Lord pleases, He does, In heaven and in earth, in the seas and in all deeps.*
>
> *Psalms 135:5, 6*

He is holy and He is perfect. He does not make mistakes:
> *And one called out to another and said, "Holy, Holy, Holy,*
> *is the Lord of hosts, the whole earth is full of His glory"*
> Isaiah 6:3

> *Therefore you are to be perfect, as your heavenly Father is*
> *perfect.*
> Matthew 5:48

Either this God we claim to serve is as these verses describe Him or He is not. Do you believe He is the only God, the Creator, all-powerful, and perfect? I recognize how basic this is, but that is step one in coming to a place where you can really trust Him without fear.

Understanding How God Feels About Us

If we are convinced that God's character, power, and personality are as described, the next important issue is to understand how this same God feels about us. After all, we are but specks in a great mass of humanity and in a vast universe. Do we make any difference to God? Again, Scripture gives us an answer.

> *Why do you say, O Jacob, and assert, O Israel, "My way*
> *is hidden from the Lord, And the justice due me escapes the*
> *notice of my God"? Do you not know? Have you not heard?*
> *The Everlasting God, the Lord, the creator of the ends of the*
> *earth Does not become weary or tired. His understanding is*
> *inscrutable.*
> Isaiah 40:27, 28

These verses tell us that in spite of the vast number of people who live or ever have lived or will live, God does not lose track of you and me!

Matthew 10:30 tells us, "The very hairs of your head are all numbered." Every time we brush our hair we can be reminded that God has just recomputed all those lost hairs—and furthermore, He knows which numbers were lost—and He is keeping a running total at all times! Who else would care how many hairs are on our heads? This gives us some idea of how much God cares for us.

In Matthew 10:29 and 31 we read that even the sparrows—those plentiful, common birds we see all the time—are under the care of God. He knows each one that falls to the ground. Can we not believe that if God cares so much about sparrows, He cares much more about us?

Psalms 139:1–3 reiterates that God cares intimately for each of us:

> *O Lord, Thou has searched me and known me. Thou dost know when I sit down and when I rise up; Thou dost understand my thought from afar. Thou dost scrutinize my path and my lying down, And art intimately acquainted with all my ways.*

Would even our mothers care to know how many times we sit down or stand up today? Yet God cares, and He knows and understands even our far-off thoughts—the ones we do not understand ourselves. He is intimately acquainted and concerned with everything we do, every place we go. If we believe the Scriptures we've quoted, we must believe this.

The God we worship, the one and only God, the eternal God, the God of all power, wisdom and holiness—this very God really cares about you and me with a care and concern unsurpassed by any other person in the world.

Understanding God's Plan for Us

God's plans for us are always superior to any other plans. If you believe those first two principles, you cannot logically deny this one. Therefore, you can trust Him. Not only *can* you trust Him, it is the only logical thing to do. Nothing else makes any sense.

Just look at what the Scriptures tell us about God's intentions toward us:

> . . . *No good thing does He withhold from those who walk uprightly.*
>
> *Psalms 84:11*

> *Now to Him who is able to do exceeding abundantly beyond all that we ask or think, according to the power that works within us.*
>
> *Ephesians 3:20*

> . . . *For to those who fear Him, there is no want. . . . But they who seek the Lord shall not be in want of any good thing.*
>
> *Psalms 34:9, 10*

The irrefutable, logical conclusion is clear. There simply can be no middle ground. If we believe with our hearts, not just our heads, that God is God, eternal, all-powerful, holy and perfect, and that this very God cares for us more than any earthly being could ever care, and that His plans for our lives are far better than anything we could engineer on our own, there can be no fear on our part to trust Him. He can be nothing but trustworthy. He will lead us into the best paths. To fail to relinquish the control of our lives to Him would be foolhardy and disastrous.

If this is so simple and so logical, why are so many Christians still refusing to really trust God, as I did for many years? I think it's because we become victims of conflicting messages from our three enemies: the world, the flesh, and the devil.

The world tells us: "Do your own thing," "Find yourself," "Do what feels good," "Go for it!" The flesh says to us: "You deserve happiness and you have a right to run your life the way you want it." The devil says: "If you trust God, you most surely will be led into a terrible life."

We listen to these voices, and we forsake consistent study of God's Word and prayer, and fear takes over. We become convinced that totally trusting God is too risky. It is meant only for those few people who somehow have the courage to go into "full-time Christian service." Without realizing what we are doing, our actions say that we believe we can trust ourselves better than we can trust God.

I am beginning to realize what arrogance it is on my part to refuse to trust God. If I really believe the three basic principles outlined above, to fail to trust Him at every turn in my life is a grave and serious sin. It is pride at its very worst.

Comprehending how totally trustworthy God is leads us to yield to His total Lordship in our lives. And this takes the monkey off our back! It gives us a marvelous freedom, because we are no longer responsible for managing our own destinies. Someone far more qualified is now in charge—the God of all the ages—and we can be absolutely sure that whatever He asks will be the best thing for us.

Finding Our Ultimate Identity

I made up my mind that Jesus Christ was worthy of my total commitment, and regardless of the cost, He would take first place. My identity began to change: No longer did I think of myself as a woman with several roles to blend and balance, switching identities like hats. But I saw myself as a woman with one obligation: to be what God wanted me to be. The identity crisis began to come to an end.

Oh, I still had to go to work every day, and I was still a woman and a mother. The roles had not gone away. But they fell into order as I began to put into practice what I had known for a long time—that I was bought with a price, I belonged to Jesus, I was not my own, and my identity was simply to be an obedient servant of my Lord.

This certainly did not all happen overnight. It was—and is—a continuing process. But it began with that moment when I gave my will over to Him, and decided that I could truly trust Him with my future—and with my identity.

This has made sweeping changes in all my roles. As I began, little by little, to apply what I was learning from my walk with God to my everyday job, that job took on a new significance. It was a part of God's plan for me and no longer a separate, sectionalized part of my life. So, I could trust God with all the details of my job and my career.

I wanted to be a better mother than ever before, and my daughter, who is now in college, has confirmed to me many times that the improvement in my mothering responsibilities has been significant. She now has a role model more important than that of a successful career woman; she now sees a mother who is learning how to let Jesus control every part of her life.

Instead of trying to find myself as a woman, my desire is to be a "woman after God's own heart." I began to learn that Jesus was very capable of filling the role of the man in my life that I felt was so necessary to fulfillment as a woman.

An End to the Struggle

Are you struggling with your identity? Do you see yourself as a person with several roles, trying to play a balancing act in prioritizing them? And plagued with guilt and frustration because you know you are not succeeding too well? Is your identity out of focus and are you wearing hats that aren't very comfortable—maybe some you know you should not be wearing at all?

Well, I want to encourage you, because there is an answer. It is the same answer it has been for ages past—and it is equally as effective for the special needs of working women as it is for everyone else.

Here it is, very simply. All of those multiple roles you're struggling with have to be replaced by one single identity—that of a woman who desires to be only and exactly what God has planned for her to be. That means giving up your will, and trusting the God of the universe with your life and your future. When you do this, the other roles will take their proper place. Jesus knows how important it is to you to be successful in your job, and in all the other areas of your life. He does not condemn you for that. It's just that He knows that unless He is the center of your life, you are headed for disappointment, confusion, and failure.

Your identity crisis ends when you identify Jesus Christ as the central focus of your life and determine that all other roles must come under His management and His direction.

That's the basic principle that began to change my life, and I am confident it will work for you, too. And when that commitment to Jesus Christ is in place, there are answers for the many confusing struggles we encounter as working women.

It is my earnest prayer that if you are experiencing this fear of trusting God, and if you are confused about your identity, you will just now relinquish your will to our loving, all-powerful God, who longs to be gracious to you and waits to have compassion on you.

Chapter Two

Self-Esteem —
Making the Most
of Your Talents

An examination of self-identity quite naturally leads to thoughts of self-esteem. Women have credits to their names that were undreamed of a generation ago. We have successes to talk about that our mothers could never have imagined. By the world's standards, we've made considerable progress on all fronts, having been "liberated" from our limited, confining roles and allowed to pursue most any that suit our fancy. How then do we regard ourselves?

Well, just recently I read a survey showing that low self-esteem is the most prevalent problem among American women today. In the early 1960s when Betty Friedan wrote *The Feminine Mystique*, she proclaimed that our low self-esteem was due to our limited roles and opportunities. Her basic message was that if women were allowed to be more than wives and mothers and could achieve identities of their own instead of simply sharing the identity of their husband, or even their children, then they would no longer feel the frustration of low self-esteem. You and I have watched the opportunities open up. But frustration is still with us. In fact the level of self-esteem has gone down rather than up in the last two decades.

What Is Self-Esteem?

First, let's define what we mean by self-esteem. We have opinions of other people, and when that opinion is positive and good, we say that we hold that person in high esteem. Conversely, we can have negative opinions of people that cause us to hold them in low esteem.

Consciously, or unconsciously, we also have an opinion of ourselves. And that opinion is our self-esteem. Opinions, as we all know, are not necessarily based on facts. The dictionary says that an *opinion* is a "conclusion or judgment held with confidence, but falling short of positive knowledge." So, the opinion we have of ourselves—our self-esteem—can be accurate, or inaccurate.

What Is Your Own Self-Esteem?

What is your opinion of yourself? If there were such a thing as a scale of self-esteem, where would you fit in? Would you be on the low end, with your head hung low, feeling totally worthless and a complete failure? Or would you find yourself at the other end, with head held high, proud of your accomplishments, confident that you can do anything you want to do, unafraid to tackle anything, assertive, successful, and proud of it? Quite likely you fall at some point in between those two descriptions. Are you in negative territory or positive territory? I'm asking you to rate your opinion of yourself, whether accurate or not. Many times we hold onto inaccurate opinions, even while recognizing some of their inaccuracies.

What Has Formed Your Self-Esteem?

Our opinions on any given subject have been shaped by various factors. They may have been formed over a long period of time or short. They may be based on good input—accurate information—or bad input—inaccurate information. They may be right or wrong conclusions. But something has influenced those opinions.

Self-Esteem Can Be Based on Comparisons

Frequently, self-esteem is based on comparisons. We compare ourselves with what we think we should be, what others have told us we should be, what society thinks we should be. A great portion of our self-esteem is based on comparison—with some other person or standard.

Now, think: To what or whom do you compare yourself? Do you look at all the so-called beautiful women today, as displayed by television and Hollywood, and conclude that all beautiful women are thin? Therefore, since you are not thin, you are not beautiful? Is that a standard of comparison you use? Do you compare yourself with what your parents said you should be? Do you compare yourself with a friend, someone at work, society's current image of the successful working woman?

Self-Esteem Can Be Based on What Others Have Told Us About Ourselves

Part of our opinion of ourselves is based on what others have told us. This could be nonverbal as well as verbal, since their actions may have told us what their words did not.

Did your parents give you lots of praise and good feelings about yourself; or did they constantly belittle you and criticize you? Or something in between? Have you had a boss who has really raised your self-esteem by telling you what a good worker you are? Or to the contrary? Do you have a husband who thinks you "hung the moon," as we say in the South, or one who is never happy with what you do?

My friend Alice's mother was extremely capable. Whatever her mother attempted, she excelled in, and she criticized everything Alice tried to do. And throughout her childhood my friend was continually reminded that what she did could have been done better by her mother.

Not surprisingly, Alice grew up with serious doubts about her ability to do things well. Her self-esteem was greatly affected by this verbal—and nonverbal—input from her mother.

Conversely, my father has always told me he thought I was capable of being anything I wanted to be. As a result, I've always been eager to try new things. His verbal positive input has made a difference in my self-esteem.

All of this input from other people goes into formulating your opinions about yourself.

Self-Esteem Can Be Based on Our Experiences

Did you win the title of "Most Likely To Succeed" when you graduated from high school? That experience could contribute favorably to your self-esteem. Did you make good grades in college? That influences your self-esteem. Did you get fired from a job? Such an experience and other failures and successes are all part of the process that creates your opinion of yourself.

I hope you have a clear understanding of what self-esteem is, and if you've never thought about it before, that you're beginning to get a picture of what has formed your present state of self-esteem—whether it is low, high, or something in between.

Why Is Low Self-Esteem at Epidemic Levels Among Women Today?

We mentioned earlier that low self-esteem is called the most prevalent problem of women today. Why would that be true, in a period when we should feel better about ourselves because of all our new accomplishments and opportunities? In thinking about it, I have come to believe that the following factors play a large part in this problem of low self-esteem among women:

1. The Superwoman Complex   Much more is expected of women today. The Superwoman Complex has hit hard. Whereas in the past society was perfectly accepting of us if we were housewives and mothers, or perhaps in some acceptable female occupation such as teacher, nurse, secretary, librarian, and so forth, now those accomplishments are not considered nearly as commendable. Indeed, what was a short time ago a perfectly acceptable standard for performance for a woman has now become almost an indictment. "You only want to be a mother and wife?" "You aren't interested in being a vice-president?" The standards to which we compare ourselves are more stringent and demanding.

Furthermore, we're expected to do what we did before in addition to taking on these many new roles open to us. This Superwoman phenomenon has gotten to many of us and has negatively affected our self-esteem.

2. Divorce   With the divorce rate increasing as it has over the past two decades, many women's self-esteem has suffered considerably. Divorce is tough! You feel as though you're wearing a sign around your neck that says, "I'm a failure: a failure at the thing which I should excel in—being a wife." And for the women who experienced rejection with their divorce—when their husband has left them for someone else—this is doubly damaging to their self-esteem.

3. Abused and Battered Women   I've read that we can expect from 25 to 50 percent of women to experience some kind of abuse in their lives. It is estimated that one out of four children suffers abuse today. Boys are abused, too, but girls are more common targets. Certainly, abuse and violence in general have increased in our society, and women are easy targets. Perhaps our new assertiveness has threatened men more than before, and that has been part of the cause for the increase in abuse—whether sexual or physical or emotional.

Without question, this sad situation has had devastating effects on the women who've experienced abuse. I'm just beginning to realize the terrible pain and suffering many women—women we personally know—have suffered through abuse.

4. The Single Syndrome   And then, more of us are single than ever before. We marry later, more of us don't marry, more of us are taking care of ourselves, no longer sharing the identity of a man. And yet our society still looks at an unmarried woman as slightly inferior—not quite making it. There is a stigma for the single woman, especially in Christian circles. Frankly, I think single women are as much the cause as the victim of that stigma, because *we* keep thinking of ourselves as incomplete unless married. And we keep behaving in ways that say to the world, "I'm desperate; I need a husband." Many single women live with this gnawing feeling inside that until they get married, they fall short of acceptable standards of success as women. And that can have very negative effects on our self-esteem.

5. Sexual Permissiveness   Another important reason for our declining self-esteem is the new sexual freedom that has become prevalent in the last few decades. No longer is it necessary for any commitment to exist in a sexual relationship. Not only is marriage not considered necessary, no type of commitment is required. God's principle of limiting sexual relationships to those who are married is now considered absolutely unreasonable and outdated by our society.

This sexual permissiveness goes totally against the nature

of women, in my opinion. Whether we admit it or not, our inborn reaction and inclination is that when we give ourselves to a man in a physical relationship, we give our hearts and our emotions, and we expect and need commitment from that man in return.

Women today, in trying to be "with it," try to ignore these natural reactions and needs, and give themselves indiscriminately, without any commitment. I believe this tears at women's self-esteem with devastating effects. The lack of any commitment or long-term relationship in these physical involvements, while quite acceptable in today's environment, does not enhance a woman's self-esteem. It causes women to lose self-respect and to lower their opinion of themselves.

6. The "Me Generation"   And then, of great significance to my mind is the fact that for the past few decades our society has been inundated with the humanistic point of view. And that humanism has caused us to focus our attention almost exclusively on ourselves. There's no question about it, we are the "Me Generation." We want to do what's right for us, we want to do our own thing, we want to grab all the gusto while we go around once. We have become extremely self-absorbed.

That self-absorption is very appealing to our human nature, and we've all been caught up in it. As we have begun to focus all our attention on ourselves—what we need, what we want, who we want to be—instead of increasing our self-esteem, we have seen the opposite effect. We think of ourselves more than ever before, we investigate ourselves more than ever before, we place an extremely high importance on ourselves and our well-being. And as we've begun focusing more and more on ourselves, we've become more and more vulnerable to our own failures, our own inadequacies, the bad breaks we've had in life or the unfair treatment we've received. All of these things take on a greater and greater significance as we concentrate more and more on ourselves. And the result? An increased negative effect on our self-esteem.

We can see how all these forces combine to create an atmosphere conducive to a lowering of women's self-esteem. But the question remains, what can we do to reverse this trend?

Solving the Problem of Low Self-Esteem

The word *self-esteem* does not appear in the Bible. Does that mean that the Bible has nothing to say about it? I believe with all my heart that God's Word is relevant to every issue we face as working women. Do you believe that too? Does it hold true for this problem of low self-esteem?

Well, since God put us all together, I believe He understands us better than anyone. Therefore, His Book should be the very best source there is on anything having to do with us as individuals. I believe the Bible has some very good answers for us. I'd like to look at the six causes of low self-esteem that I've listed, and see what the Word of God has to tell us about each of them.

1. The Superwoman Complex What is the root cause of the Superwoman Complex? I believe it results from comparing ourselves to what we think we should be or what society tells us we should be. We try to be superwomen because we've been convinced that the acceptable standard

for women today is to be able to do anything and everything, and to do it very well. We've compared ourselves
with other people and other standards, and decided that in
order to be acceptable, we have to be superwomen.

Do you do that? Do you come up on the short end? Are
you aware that as a Christian woman, it is wrong for you to
compare yourself with other people?

Remember what Jesus taught us. After the resurrection,
when Jesus prophesied to Peter that he would be called on
to suffer for Him, Peter turned and looked at John and said,
"What about him?" Jesus said to Peter, "What is that to
you? Follow thou me" (see John 21:21, 22). Jesus is clearly
telling Peter not to compare himself with others. The same
is true for us today. Jesus would say to us, "What difference
does that make to you? Your job is to follow me, without
comparing your circumstances, your abilities, your position,
your background, your education, your age, your looks—or
anything else, with anyone else. Your duty is simply to follow me."

And then He gave us another clear message in the parable
of the talents (see Matthew 25:14–28). I'm going to examine
this parable in some detail because it is also relevant to
other areas of discussion in this book.

As he was leaving on a journey, a master left his three
servants with different talents. To one he gave five talents,
to one two, and to the other one he gave one talent. The
servant with the five talents went right to work and doubled
his talents to ten. Likewise, the servant with two talents
doubled his talents to four. But the servant with one talent
reacted quite differently. He went away and dug a hole in
the ground and buried his one talent.

I believe it's quite likely that this man with one talent was jealous and miffed because he had only one talent and the others had more. I think he made a comparison and felt cheated because he didn't start out with as much as the others. And that comparison could have caused him to lose confidence in himself. Don't you imagine that he might well have felt very inadequate about having only one talent, and doubted his ability to be able to do anything with his one little talent? I really believe this servant was suffering from low self-esteem.

Well, what happens when the master returns? He calls these servants to account for what they've done with their talents. The first two report that they have doubled their money. One now has ten talents, the other now has four. The master gives to each of them the exact same reply:

"Well done, good and faithful slave; you were faithful with a few things, I will put you in charge of many things; enter into the joy of your master" (Matthew 25:23).

Even though one slave had more than twice what the other slave had, they got the same reward and the same commendation. That master didn't say, "Well, the ten-talent slave is obviously better than the four-talent slave, because he has more talents. Therefore, he gets first place and the four-talent guy gets second place." He did not compare their results or demand that the two-talent servant do as much as the five-talent servant did. Because both of them had diligently done well with what they started with, they were regarded as being equally successful.

But notice our one-talent servant—the one who went out and buried his money. When the master asked him for a report, here's what he said:

> *Master, I knew you to be a hard man, reaping where you did not sow, and gathering where you scattered no seed. And*

I was afraid, and went away and hid your talent in the ground; see, you have what is yours.

Matthew 25:24, 25

Does his answer make sense to you? This poor servant was not thinking very straight. He knows his master is interested in increasing his money, but instead of doing what he knows will please the master, he hides the money. He's so afraid of losing that one talent, he buries it.

Now, if you didn't know the rest of this parable, and you were to write the ending, what would you write? I think most of us would write something like this: "Oh, well, that's okay. I know how you feel. And besides you just had one talent anyway—it's no big deal. But listen, next time why don't you look at what these other fellows did and try to be more like them. You need to try a little harder next time."

Let me quote the ending that Jesus gave to this story:

You wicked, lazy slave, you knew that I reap where I did not sow, and gather where I scattered no seed. Then you ought to have put my money in the bank, and on my arrival I would have received my money back with interest. Therefore take away the talent from him, and give it to the one who has the ten talents.

Matthew 25:26–28

What? He called this fellow wicked and lazy! Can you imagine? No sympathy whatsoever for the fact that he had only one talent to begin with. And why is he upset over one silly talent? After all, the other two servants earned an additional seven talents for him.

What is the principle that Jesus is teaching us here? Look at it very carefully because it is most important:

Jesus does not compare us with other people. His standard of acceptable performance is that we take what we have been given and we do a lot with it. His rewards and commendations are not based on how much we accomplish, how far up the ladder we climb, but rather they are based on comparing where we started with where we finish.

When we compare ourselves with other people, other criteria, other standards, we will become demoralized and frustrated. Like the man with one talent, we'll give up before we get started. We'll just tuck our tails between our legs, and go home and sit and wait.

You are responsible to your Master to multiply the talents you've been given, but He will not compare your results with those of other people. What He expects of me is not what He expects of you in actual results. But He does expect all of us to multiply our talents, whatever they are.

Jesus gave us this powerful illustration so that we will understand His priorities and standards of performance. He will have no sympathy for the less-talented, less-educated person who uses that as an excuse to bury herself and do nothing. He will have no sympathy for the person who uses her bad background or bad breaks as an excuse for sitting home and feeling sorry for herself. But He does not expect a one-talent person to do what the five-talent person does.

By the same token, we can compare ourselves with others and decide we're pretty "hot stuff." You know, we can always find someone lower on the totem pole than we are. And if we make comparisons of that sort, we can make the mistake of thinking more highly of ourselves than we

should. Then, taking our leisure like the rabbit in the fa-
mous race with the turtle, we, also, will fail to use our talents properly. Jesus taught us that to whom much is given,
much is required (Luke 12:48).

As long as we keep comparing ourselves to other people
and their standards, our self-esteem will never be healthy. It
will either be too low or too high. But by taking the abilities
and opportunities given to us and multiplying whatever
they are, we'll find that our opinion of ourselves will become more accurate and realistic—and healthier.

2. Divorce For those of you who, like me, have gone
through a divorce, I have good news. It is *not* the unpardon-
able sin. Whatever the reason or cause of your divorce,
whether it was your idea or not, as long as you've confessed
any sin on your part, you are not condemned by the Lord.
In fact, He says He doesn't even remember our sins once
they are confessed. And hold on to this wonderful verse,
Isaiah 61:3:

> *To appoint unto them that mourn in Zion, to give unto them*
> *beauty for ashes, the oil of joy for mourning, the garment of*
> *praise for the spirit of heaviness; that they might be called*
> *Trees of righteousness, The planting of the Lord, that he*
> *might be glorified.* (KJV)

Your ashes can be turned into beauty, your mourning
into joy. That heavy spirit you carry around with you can
become a spirit of praise. And you—yes you, a divorced
woman—can be called a tree of righteousness, you can become the Lord's plant, and He will be glorified through you.

Ask God to help you shed the heavy garment of failure

that we divorced people tend to wear. God is no respecter of persons. He doesn't favor a nondivorced person over a divorced person. Your life is not ruined. You can become what God wants you to be. Oh, do believe this.

And if you experienced rejection as a result of that divorce, remember this. Jesus Christ has promised never to leave you or forsake you. NEVER. Now, consider how special you are, that Jesus Christ will never leave you. I know how that rejection hurts, but Jesus can heal it. Wrap yourself in His love, and constantly think of the fact that He will always be with you. Nothing will ever separate you from Christ, if you know Him as your Savior.

Concentrating on Christ's love for you can heal those wounds caused by divorce and rejection, and can restore your self-esteem to an acceptable level.

3. Abused and Battered Women   If you are a part of those statistics on abused and battered women, my heart reaches out to you with great compassion. I can only imagine how deep the scars must be and how difficult it is to find healing and relief.

I know that most abused women are made to believe that they suffered that abuse because they were worthless, even bad, people. One of the biggest hurdles for abused women is that gnawing feeling that they deserve what happened to them, that there was some evil in them that caused the abuse.

The healing you need is not a quick fix, I know that. That's why we have to establish support groups on a long-term basis. You may well need some professional help from a Christian counselor, as well, to be able to deal with your memories and your past.

I would just say to you, as one Christian woman to another, that I know you can find healing in Jesus. I know that He understands your suffering, that God is outraged at what happened to you.

Meanwhile, you must cope with the damage that abuse has done to your opinion of yourself, your self-esteem. My best advice to you is to saturate yourself with the Word of God. As I've talked to women who have experienced abuse, I realize that those who have really spent time in God's Word are far more capable of recovering from the damage done to them than those who have not.

It will do several things for you. It will show you how much God loves you and how important you are to Him. And it will give you a basis for reprogramming your mind. Your memories and your thinking need to be reprogrammed, and God's Word is the best input for that.

Remember, God sees you as a pure, lovely creature, made by Him in a special way. The abuse you may have suffered has not caused Him to find you unlovely or unlovable. He affirms you as a woman whom He loves, and He cares intimately about you. I know that as you can begin to find your completeness in Him, He will have healing for those terrible hurts. And He can heal the damage done to your self-esteem. There's nothing too hard for our God. And He longs to be gracious to you.

4. The Single Syndrome If, because you are single, you have the uneasy feeling that you're not quite a real person yet, your self-esteem has undoubtedly suffered as a result. Now, I truly understand this, because I spent the first ten years after my divorce struggling with this feeling of inadequacy because I wasn't married. I felt that if I could marry the kind of man I sought, everybody would sit up and take notice and say, "Wow, Mary Whelchel must be really something. Look at the man who married her." I wanted a man to wear as my badge of acceptability. My self-esteem was suffering, and I was certain that the right man was the cure for that problem.

Let me tell you briefly what I have learned. There is not a man on earth who can give you the total affirmation that you are looking for. You can ask the most happily married woman you know, and she will tell you, if she is honest, that there are many times that her husband does not and cannot meet her needs.

The only man who can give you complete affirmation is the Man, Christ Jesus. If you really want a badge to wear, wear His badge. How much better can you get? To say you belong to Him has to be the best credentials you can ever have.

I see so many single women doing what I did for so long, and my heart breaks for them. I know you're looking for acceptance, but I so want you to believe me when I tell you that you don't have to be married to be fulfilled as a woman.

Listen to what the Apostle Paul tells us in 1 Corinthians 7:34:

> And the woman who is unmarried, and the virgin, is concerned about the things of the Lord, that she may be holy both in body and spirit; but one who is married is concerned about the things of the world, how she may please her husband.

To get the full context of that verse, you need to read that whole chapter. Paul doesn't condemn marriage, but he does tell us that we have more freedom when we are not married.

Would any married woman deny that fact? And Paul is telling us that to remain unmarried can indeed be very praiseworthy and honorable.

Why is it we never look at this Scripture and concentrate on its truth? Yes, marriage is a wonderful thing. Yes, the family is the basic building block of our society. But that does not mean that the unmarried have less credibility or purpose. *Just the opposite!* We should be able to be more concerned about eternal matters because we are not married.

If you're a single Christian woman, burdened with the image of yourself as "Incomplete Until Married," please read this chapter in 1 Corinthians again and again and believe its truth. You can be so very special in God's kingdom. Hold your head high and declare yourself married to the Lord, and go forward. You're not just okay; you're special!

5. Sexual Permissiveness It's my opinion that many women have suffered a great deal of damage to their self-esteem because of their permissive attitude toward sexual relationships with men. I know that this is perfectly acceptable in many segments of our society today. But it is not acceptable by God's principles. Sex is reserved for marriage. And not because God is a gigantic killjoy, who wants to make our life difficult. But because He knows that this intimate relationship, apart from commitment, can do nothing but harm us. And you can see that very thing happening to women all around you, maybe even to you.

When a woman gives herself physically without the commitment of marriage, she not only is committing a sin, she is dealing death blows to her self-esteem. It may not seem so at first. The attention may cause you to think that you're really special for a while. But before it's over, you'll suffer greatly from these illegitimate relationships. God's principles are for our good, not to make life difficult. There is only one answer to this problem: Determine to live a life of purity, regardless of the price you must pay. It will bring healing to your damaged self-esteem.

6. The "Me Generation" I think all of us have to plead guilty to the problem of being self-absorbed. First, we're born that way. Ever notice that you didn't have to teach your children to be selfish? They come by it naturally. And second, our particular generation has had a double-whammy of self-absorption because of the current trend toward humanistic thinking.

Biblical principles are exactly opposite to this intense concentration on who we are, what makes us tick, and taking care of number one.

> *Jesus said to His disciples, "If anyone would come after Me, let him deny himself, and take up his cross and follow Me."*
> *Matthew 16:24*

> *For through the grace given to me I say to every man among you not to think more highly of himself than he ought to think; but to think so as to have sound judgment, as God has allotted to each a measure of faith.*
> *Romans 12:3*

> *Do nothing from selfishness or empty conceit, but with humility of mind let each of you regard one another as more important than himself.*
> *Philippians 2:3*

Rather than telling us how to improve our self-esteem, Jesus tells us to deny ourselves. Rather than dressing up this old self of ours and showing everyone how wonderful we are, Jesus tells us to die to ourselves. There is nothing in the teaching of our Master that would cause us to pursue a course of promoting our own selves. He taught us to be servants, as He was a servant.

I think it is a mistake to concentrate on our self-esteem. Now don't get me wrong—I don't mean that self-esteem should go away. You will always have an opinion of yourself. And that opinion needs to be realistic and positive. But we need to get out of ourselves, stop concentrating on ourselves, and start investing our lives in other people.

We do need self-acceptance. We need to love ourselves. Jesus said we were to love our neighbors as we love ourselves. So, loving ourselves is necessary and important. We won't be able to love others until we can love ourselves.

We need to have an accurate understanding of who we are as Christian women, and base our opinions of ourselves on that understanding. God has created us in His image. Now, think about that. Further, as we read in Ephesians, because we belong to Him, we are seated in the heavenlies with Christ Jesus, we are heirs of God, and joint heirs with Jesus Christ. Think of what that means.

When I think about who I am in Jesus and because of Jesus, the rest of my background and failures starts to diminish in importance. So what, that I don't fit the world's mold of what beautiful should be! So what, if I don't measure up to someone else's standards of acceptability. So what, that I'm not a superwoman. So what, if my accomplishments are less than other women's. No one can condemn me, because Jesus doesn't condemn me. Read what Paul wrote to the Romans.

> *Who would dare to accuse us, whom God has chosen? God himself has declared us free from sin. Who is in a position to condemn? Only Christ Jesus, and Christ died for us, Christ rose for us, Christ reigns in power for us, Christ prays for us!*
>
> Romans 8:33–35 (PHILLIPS)

If someone is condemning you—or you are condemning yourself—and your self-esteem is at rock bottom because you don't think you measure up, will you memorize this Scripture and believe it? Nobody has a right to accuse you of anything—not even yourself. Nobody can accuse you except Christ. But the wonderful news is that Christ doesn't accuse you. He died for you, He rose for you, He reigns for you, He prays for you! The first verse of that same eighth chapter of Romans says that "no condemnation now hangs over the head of those who are in Christ Jesus."

Who is "in" Christ Jesus? Those who have accepted Him as their Savior. Are you in Christ Jesus? If the answer is yes, then you are not condemned by Him.

Now, based on this incredible truth, we need to accept who we are in Christ, and then move on to other things. We've got to conquer this absorption with self if we're ever going to be able to reach this world with the love of Christ.

When you leave for work in the morning, and you feel that you look terrible, what do you think about all day? You think about how you look. You keep going into the ladies' room to see if you can make your hair look better. You hate yourself for wearing a suit that looks so bad on you. All day long your thoughts are of yourself. But, when you leave home feeling that you look pretty nifty, and your hair behaves properly, and that new dress looks good, it really frees you up, doesn't it? You stop thinking about yourself, because you feel confident that you look okay.

When you start to feel confident that you are so special because you belong to the Lord Jesus, then you can start to forget yourself and reach out to others. That means that we must learn to deny ourselves, die to our own desires, think of others as more important than we are, become servants, love our neighbors as ourselves. I really believe that as we Christian women begin to tackle this problem of self-absorption, we'll begin to see dramatic improvements in our self-esteem.

One of the great paradoxes of Scripture is that when we die to ourselves, we become alive unto God. When we start to reach out to others and care about other people, regardless of how needy we may be, we're going to discover that the healing process starts. That low self-esteem problem we've been battling will never be won by getting more promotions or a face lift or losing weight or going back to school. Not that there is anything wrong with any of those things, and certainly they can help us feel better about ourselves. But they are only Band-Aids. They're not the cure.

Many of us are so crippled by low self-esteem that we can't help anyone else. We're like the man with the one talent, who sat in his corner and buried his talent, full of anger, full of envy, feeling very inadequate, and too frightened to try to do anything for fear he would lose what he had. We're useless to the purposes of God's kingdom when we're so crippled by low self-esteem. And our behavior just continues to confirm to us that we truly are not worth very much. It becomes a vicious cycle.

It makes no difference to God what you start with: How poor your background is, what failures you've had, what messes you've made, how dumb you think you are, what few abilities you may think you have are not of any importance to your Master. Wherever you are, whatever you are starting with, He expects you to go for it, and double whatever you have. Remember that the two servants who did double their talents were given more talents because of their faithfulness. If you start multiplying what you have, you'll discover that your talents increase. But if you remain a cripple to your own self-esteem, the judgment against you will be very strong.

I want to stand before God and hear, "Well done, good and faithful servant," don't you? We can, you know. Every one of us has that potential. But we must set our will and our mind to accept ourselves where we are, and then go on from there.

Chapter Three

Ambition, Success, and Money

My friend Jane, who is a nurse, recently made an unusual job change. After years of pursuing her nursing career and working diligently and successfully to be a first-rate nurse, she decided to leave nursing and become a secretary in the hospital. That move on her part meant a significant cut in salary, and in most people's view, it was a step down the career ladder. Why did she do it? Didn't she like nursing? Had she had a bad experience that soured her on her career?

No, she enjoyed nursing, and may go back to it someday. But because of the schedule required of her as a nurse, she could never take any responsibility at church and had to miss many church functions and opportunities for service. After much thought and prayer, she felt God would have her choose a different career, at least for a time, in order to free up her schedule for serving in various ministries.

Many of her friends and associates, not understanding

her motives, have questioned the wisdom of this move on her part. You see, the world expects all of us to be driven to pursue higher positions, greater success, and more money. To have a different set of ambitions and a different measurement of success is indeed unusual in our working environment.

Christians and non-Christians alike, male and female, easily become absorbed in their ambition for business success. The desire for the money and power that are available at higher levels consumes many people, and their lives revolve around their professional ambitions.

There is definitely an unspoken law in the business world that goes like this: It is normal for working people to aspire to higher levels, to seek unending promotions, and to work continually to increase their earnings. Any amount of energy and time expended to these ends is intelligent, justified, and sensible.

I have observed that this mind-set has often had two opposite and damaging effects on Christian working women. Many have bought into this ambition syndrome and have lost a proper perspective of what a Christian's priorities should be. Others, who have not been motivated to greater career ambitions, experience guilt and feelings of inadequacy because they aren't "achievers."

Let's examine both sides and try to determine how God's principles apply to this issue.

For a Christian in the working world, possessing or not possessing career ambitions is neither spiritual nor unspiritual. There is no scriptural directive that points us exclusively in either direction. Each category, however, has dangers about which you should be aware.

The Success Treadmill

Ambition

In this new era of equal opportunity, women are allowed to move ahead into jobs and positions that were closed to them only a few years ago. Indeed, we are *expected* to be ambitious, to strive for promotions, to forge new territory, and set new records.

Certainly, many of us have benefited from this new environment. I recognize that my life-style has been favorably affected by getting a job as a sales representative in a company where that job had been closed to women only a few short months before. That experience qualified me for other jobs, and the chain reaction enabled me to pursue a fairly successful career, with the monetary and ego rewards that such accomplishments bring.

I for one am very thankful for being allowed to move ahead, since by personality, I'm a competitive, energetic, achiever type. Being in a position, as a single mother, of having to work, it was in many ways a benefit to me to have the opportunity to advance. Had I been a generation older and faced similar circumstances, my options would have been greatly limited and that would have made a significant difference in my standard of living.

So, for those of us who are inclined to push ahead in the working world, these new opportunities have been appreciated. It is not my purpose to lay a guilt trip on anyone who has taken advantage of these opportunities and advanced her career as much as possible. There is nothing in Scripture that forbids or condemns career or monetary success.

It is possible to be successful in a career or professional pursuit, to receive promotions, to attain high positions, and to excel in our jobs, and be absolutely in line with God's purposes for our lives. Joseph and Daniel are two outstanding examples of very successful businessmen, used greatly by God in their positions. Lydia is another person who used her success and her position to spread the Gospel through her home into Europe. The Proverbs 31 woman had unusual business interests and success, and she is considered a role model for a godly woman.

However, the Christian who is energetically pursuing career goals needs to be very much aware of the dangers and pitfalls that exist in that high-powered environment. Let's face it, highly ambitious career-minded people are quite often workaholics. They devote inordinate amounts of time to their jobs. Frequently such a person has little time or energy left for anything else, including family, friends, church ministries, and so forth.

I could easily make a long list of people I know who have sacrificed many other important priorities in order to move their careers ahead. If they are Christians, they are not the people you call on at church to help with a project, because they never have time. If they somehow get pressured into accepting some church responsibility, they rarely fulfill their commitments because work has them tied up.

Have you noticed how often the excuse "I had to work" is used, as though there can be no contesting the fact that work must take first place. I've done it myself far too often, excusing myself from a commitment because "something came up at work." Undoubtedly there are times when it is unavoidable. But the Christian who is never available or dependable for any type of service, whether church related or not, needs to seriously consider if this job pursuit is in line with God's purpose for her life.

Now, we walk a fine line here, because in no way am I advocating lack of excellence. Excellence should be our trademark as Christians in all our endeavors. When the jobs we have taken require extra effort and overtime in order to meet a deadline or some other type of temporary emergency, we should be available for that service. However, if your job *continually* requires such a total dedication on your part that there is never time for other responsibilities, you need to do an assessment of your priorities. Or if you find yourself so eager to move ahead that you pour all your energy and vitality into your job, even though it may not be required, that is another signal that you need to stop and take your spiritual pulse and temperature. There is one directive given by our Lord that clearly defines what our priorities should be: "But seek first His kingdom and His righteousness; and all these things shall be added to you" (Matthew 6:33).

The scope of this command, and the promise given with it, is immense. Few Christians have ever dared to prove it true in their lives. What does it mean to seek first His kingdom and His righteousness? How could any of us hold down everyday "secular" jobs, which by necessity occupy most of our waking hours, and still claim to seek God's kingdom first?

At first look, it would seem impossible, wouldn't it? But earlier we talked about God's view of work, and how our jobs can be a vital part of God's plan for our lives. So, it is possible to have a job and even career ambitions and still keep our priorities in line with Matthew 6:33.

It requires a constant assessment on our part of just what

our motives are and where our priorities lie. Is our career drive simply an ego trip, something we're doing to prove that we're capable or to establish our worth? Many times Christians use their jobs as a substitute for finding their fulfillment in the Lord Jesus—the satisfaction and self-esteem that only Jesus can give.

Money

Another potential trouble area for the person on the success treadmill is the love of money. Success usually brings more money, and that money can get a grip on our lives so fast that we hardly realize it. Unquestionably, all of us work, in part, for money. If our companies did not hand us a paycheck at regular intervals, we'd soon leave the job even if we liked the work. There is no denying that we work in large part because we need money; and money is the leverage that our employers use to keep us coming back every day to work some more!

Is it wrong to work for money? No, and in fact the Bible exhorts us to earn our own way, to be industrious, and not to be dependent on others for our necessities.

> *But if any one does not provide for his own, and especially for those of his household, he has denied the faith, and is worse than an unbeliever.*
>
> 1 Timothy 5:8

> *Laziness casts into a deep sleep, and an idle man will suffer hunger.*
>
> Proverbs 19:15

Honest work for an honest paycheck is honorable. But how easily money can become our motivation. Not long ago a passage from 1 Timothy 6 really spoke to me on this matter of wanting to make a lot of money:

> There is a real profit, of course, but it comes only to those who live contentedly as God would have them live. We brought absolutely nothing with us when we entered this world, and we can be sure we shall take absolutely nothing with us when we leave it. Surely then, as far as physical things are concerned, it is sufficient to us to keep our bodies fed and clothed. For people who set their hearts on being wealthy expose themselves to temptation. They fall into one of the world's traps and lay themselves open to all sorts of silly and wicked desires, which are quite capable of utterly ruining and destroying their souls. For loving money leads to all kinds of evil, and some men in the struggle to be rich have lost their faith and caused themselves untold agonies of mind.

> But you, the man of God, keep clear of such things. Set your heart not on riches, but on goodness, Christ-likeness, faith, love, patience and humility. Fight the worth-while battle of the Faith, keep your grip on that life eternal to which you have been called, and to which you boldly professed your loyalty before many witnesses.

> Tell those who are rich in this present world not to be contemptuous of others, and not to rest the weight of their confidence on the transitory power of wealth but on the living God, Who generously gives us everything for our enjoyment. Tell them to do good, to be rich in kindly actions, to be ready

to give to others and to sympathise with those in distress.
Their security should be invested in the life to come, so that
they may be sure of holding a share in the Life which is per-
manent.

                              1 Timothy 6:6–10; 11, 12; 17–19
                                        (YOUNG CHURCHES)

When we begin to set our hearts on more money, a better
position, more status, we're setting ourselves up for spiritual failure. Paul tells young Timothy that we expose ourselves to temptation and various traps. These traps are very
deceptive and it isn't difficult to fall into them. What are
these traps waiting for those who set their hearts and ambitions on money and success?

1. *Being Contemptuous of Others*   The first one is being
contemptuous of others. We begin to think that our money
gives us higher status, more importance, and more validity
than other people. You can probably think of people
who've achieved a certain level of success and have an attitude that says, "I can't waste my time on less important
people anymore."

Becoming contemptuous is an easy trap for people who
love money because they judge people's worth by the
amount of money they earn. And that can happen to any of
us. I can remember seeing some statistics about women's
salaries a few years ago, and I became aware of my income
in relation to that of other women. I had never thought
about it before, but just seeing those statistics tended to
make me think more highly of myself. I was in a higher
bracket than I would have guessed, and my opinion of myself increased because of my income.

That's a pretty ridiculous way for a Christian to think. Scripture does not approve of this tendency on our part to judge ourselves and others by the amount of money we make. God certainly doesn't judge us that way.

Yet we see it all the time in the working world. More respect is given to the people at the top who earn big money. Their financial success impresses everyone. But remember that we look on the outward appearance, and God looks on the heart. He is *no* respecter of persons! He could not be less impressed with the dollar amount on our paychecks or in our bank accounts.

2. Confidence in the Power of Money Another trap Paul points out is that people with money put their confidence in the power of money. Frankly, even people without money do that. We think if we just had a certain income level, things would go well for us. Life's problems would go away. Very subtly we begin to look to money for our security.

As I write this, God is in the process of showing me how much I have trusted in money in the past, and how that trust has kept me from learning to trust God more completely. If you, like me, were raised with the idea that a responsible person puts money away for rainy days, has money in the bank for security in case something goes wrong, and prudently saves a nest egg to fall back on, you will likely find that you have developed a dependency upon money that is difficult to break.

Recently a friend said to me, "Mary, none of us really wants to be totally dependent upon God. We all want our security blankets tucked away in a safe place to get us through any tough spots in our lives." His words were a dagger to my heart, as I had to admit that in this financial area, I could not imagine being without a little money put back to make sure that I could take care of myself. Paul warned those who are rich or have a great desire for money not to "rest the weight of their confidence on the transitory power of wealth." How utterly ridiculous for us to put our hope of security in a little—or a large—amount of money. Money is probably the least dependable commodity in the world. There are any number of things that could happen overnight which could wipe out that money in one blow. Satan has lied to us and we've come to believe his lie that money can give us security, not to mention happiness and contentment.

Real contentment, Paul says, comes *only* to those who live as God would have them live. This trap of expecting money to bring us security and contentment is so prevalent in our society, that for me it almost seems impossible to tear it out by its roots and get it out of my life. But I challenge you, as I'm challenging myself, to prove God true, to change your thinking about money, and to examine and see where your trust really lies.

3. Self-Centeredness   Another trap we can fall into when we start focusing on earning money is that we become very self-centered. Our financial success becomes the focal point of our whole life, and little by little, other things drop off. We become absorbed with amassing riches for ourselves, and that attitude leaves little room for caring for others. Unfortunately, this attitude can creep up on us and take over without our realizing what is happening.

Paul says we are to set our hearts on goodness, Christlikeness, faith, love, patience, and humility. When our minds are focused on earning money or great success, we seldom have time to focus on the virtues that are the fruits of the Holy Spirit operating in our lives.

Think of those you know or have known who set their whole heart on money. Do you really admire them? Were they a pleasure to be with? Were they an encouragement to you? Or were they self-absorbed, frantic, pressurized people who were always in a hurry, but never with time for anyone but themselves?

Now think of someone you know who set his or her whole heart on goodness and Christ-likeness. I think of a single lady who is now retired and lives in Ohio. She has set her whole life on Christ-likeness. And every day of her life is an encouragement and a joy to others. She was in our church for many years, and I keep learning of people in the church whose lives she has profoundly affected for the glory of God.

This marvelous woman continues to set her heart on Christ-likeness and faith and love and patience and humility, and every year she is more a blessing to others than the year before. She doesn't have a lot of money. But her priorities are right on with Scripture and with the exhortation Paul gave to Timothy. She has kept her body fed and clothed very nicely through the years, but that has never been of utmost importance to her. As a result, she has been freed from all the cares that the love of money brings, all the worries and fretting and planning and figuring that happens when money is paramount. She is so much happier and freer than people I know who have lots and lots of money, that I'm sure she would never think of changing places with them.

How easy it is for us to lose sight of what is really important. And the accumulation of money is a very dangerous area for us. Yes, true, there are Christians who have a great deal of money, and who use it to the glory of God. But those people have never loved that money. And if they lost it, it would not destroy them. They know how temporary it is. They have learned the truth of Psalms 62:10: " . . . If riches increase, do not set your heart upon them." As their money has increased, they have simply used it as a gift from God for His glory.

Agur wrote in Proverbs 30:8, 9: " . . . Give me neither poverty nor riches; Feed me with the food that is my portion, Lest I be full and deny Thee and say, 'Who is the Lord?' Or lest I be in want and steal, And profane the name of my God."

Jesus told the disciples, "It is easier for a camel to go through the eye of a needle, than for a rich man to enter the kingdom of God" (Matthew 19:24). It is the rare Christian who can handle great financial success well. The traps are many, and the temptations are constant. More often than not, having money ruins a person's commitment to Jesus Christ, rather than enhances it. It doesn't have to be that way, but sadly, it often is.

On God's balance sheet, things look a lot different than they do in our checkbooks. He looks on the asset side for goodness, faith, love, patience, humility, Christ-likeness. This is what is important to Him.

So, if you're building your working life around a desire to get ahead and earn lot of money, stop and check it out. The evils that it could lead you into are many. And in the end, how much money you make or have is absolutely unimportant to God. He looks at the set of your heart, and searches for those who hunger and thirst for righteousness. He has promised that they will be satisfied. But money will never satisfy anyone.

Again, as Christians in a working world, we have an opportunity to shine as lights in darkness if we exhibit a different attitude about money. If those around us can see that money is not our prime motivator, that we trust in God more than we trust in money, they have to take notice of that attitude. That is the kind of salt that makes people thirsty for the water that we have.

What? No Career Ambitions?

But what about the women whose ambitions lie in other directions, and have no desire to build outstanding careers or be super businesswomen?

One of the negative results of this new era of women's rights has been that many women feel guilty because they don't feel a compulsion to climb a career ladder. Many force themselves to try, because of the pressure they feel from society. Then failure or lack of great success can bring a real self-image problem. It seems to be a no-win situation for many women.

While many have seen this new environment as challenging and stimulating, a great many others feel caught in the middle. Because they don't have career ambitions, they somehow feel guilty and apologetic, as though they have failed as women.

It is amazing to me to observe the changes in the nature of the dilemmas faced by women, even in my short lifetime. When I graduated from high school, not that many years ago, I was expected to want to be a wife and mother. A college education was nice, but no one considered it terribly necessary for a woman.

Had I, in the early 1960's, expressed an ambition to become a vice-president of a large corporation, I would have received little support or encouragement. I would have been the exception, not the rule, and there would have been a struggle because that ambition deviated from the norm.

Just a few years later, my daughter, in her freshman year at college, having to pick her major subject, felt a great pressure to have definite career ambitions. At the age of eighteen she felt that she was expected to have a plan for her life very clearly in mind, with goals and objectives that would lead her to an acceptable, successful career. Some of that pressure must have been a result of having a single, career mother as a role model for the past ten years. But such pressure is not unique to my daughter; most girls in high school and college have the subconscious, if not conscious, notion that they must aspire to be more than a housewife, more than a mother. Anything less would denote lack of ambition, lack of intelligence, and a serious deviation from the norm.

Society is beginning to take note of this backlash caused by the feminist movement and the guilt it has placed on many women who do not choose to pursue careers or professions. Have you noticed how the pendulum of social change makes great wide sweeps from one side of the spectrum to the other, only briefly touching middle ground as it moves?

You may have noticed that lately many television news specials have focused on the woman who has chosen to stay home with her children, forsaking or postponing her career while they are young. Twenty years ago the specials would have highlighted the woman who chose to forgo family pursuits for the corporate world. We've seen, and lived through, dramatic changes in public awareness and expectations for women in the last two decades.

Little wonder that many women have been caught in this pendulum swing, finding it difficult to distinguish their own true ambitions from what is expected of them. As is so often the case, we've again thrown the baby out with the water, but this time the analogy is sadly close to reality.

Well, where does that leave us as Christian women if we do not aspire to great career heights, yet are a part of the working world? What do we do about these guilt feelings, about the pressure we feel from society to be superwomen, excelling at everything we do?

The lack of career ambitions does not mean the lack of all ambitions or the lack of proper ambitions. God measures success quite differently from the world's measurements, and a Christian who has no desire to achieve new heights in the working world need feel no guilt for that lack of ambition. Though the "system" seems to say that all worthy people have ambitions to get ahead in their jobs, that is not a biblical principle, and the Christian working person need not take on the guilt that Satan and his system would lay on us.

Wife and Mother

If you choose or have chosen to be a wife and mother, and you now have children in your home, it is clear from

Scripture that your priority must always be the welfare of your children. If your ambitions are to be the best mom and wife possible, you're in safe spiritual territory. Nothing is more important. Careers always should take a backseat for a Christian mother. So, lift your head high when you have an opportunity to tell someone that your top priority is your children and your home, and your career goals are not more important. Never be ashamed of that. It is a wise and intelligent lady who keeps those priorities in line.

Job Performance

The person who does not have career ambitions needs to be careful of certain pitfalls, however. As long as you work for someone and receive a salary, you are responsible for giving excellent service. While you may not be trying to win any promotions, as a Christian you are commanded to do your work to the best of your ability. Lack of any ambition to advance your career can cause you to lose your drive for excellence. That should never be true of a Christian. Jesus was an extra-miler all the way, in everything He did. We must be careful not to damage the testimony of Christ through sloppy or mediocre work.

Think back to or reread our discussion of the parable of the talents from Matthew 25:14–28. I believe this parable also has much to offer us on what Jesus thinks about ambition and success.

I believe the first benefit we can gain from understanding this parable is that not all of us are endowed with equal talents and abilities. Have you ever tried to make an objective assessment of whether you are a five-talent, two-talent, or one-talent person—or something in between? Maturity, I am learning, helps us to realize, perhaps painfully at first, that certain gifts and abilities are ours within limits and certain others have been denied us altogether. This parable teaches us that the important issue is not how talented or gifted we are. After all, we really had nothing to do with the abundance of our talent, or lack of it.

We are not judged by what we start with in the matter of talents. If you do not have a great store of abilities, if you do not have unusual brain power or if you do not naturally possess the mental quickness or agility to be a top executive, you do not have to feel guilty or abnormal. You will never be judged or condemned by God based on the amount of talent you have to start with.

Now, that alone is a very freeing thought. Regardless of what society may expect, you have one Master who really matters, Jesus Christ, and He tells you clearly here that for reasons you may not understand, some of us have fewer talents than others. We really need to make an assessment of our abilities, objectively, and accept whatever level it is that is our beginning place.

We know that God is not a respecter of persons. Therefore, He does not prefer a five-talent person over a two-talent person, or a two-talent person over a one-talent person. Remember that the two-talent person, who although he doubled his money, still had less than half of what the five talent person had, received the same exact commendation from the master. There was no difference in their rewards.

Since the five-talent servant had more to begin with, the master expected him to produce more. The fact that he had much more than the other two was of no special significance to the master. It was what he had done with what he had that was important. Ask God to help you make an honest assessment of your talent and ability level, knowing that the number of talents you have to begin with is not the important issue at all. Once you can look at yourself and say, "I'm a two-talent, average, middle-of-the-road person," or, "I'm a five-talent, highly gifted person," or "My gifts are fewer than most, I'm a one-talent person," then you are free from having to be anything except what you are. With that assessment in your mind, the next question is tougher. What have you done with the talents given to you?

Notice the outrage of the master when he learns that the one-talent servant has not multiplied his talent. Why should the master be so outraged? We're only talking about one small talent here, and from his other two servants he has increased his possessions by seven talents already.

Why would the lack of this one talent be so important? It is Jesus' way again of showing us the importance He places on small service. He has told us that a cup of cold water given in His name will be remembered; He said the poor widow's mite was a greater gift than all the large offerings of the religious hypocrites; He said that when we do good to one small, insignificant person, we do it to Him. It is God, not our human wisdom, who determines whether a gift is great or small.

Therefore, what the one-talent person did with his talent was just as important to the master as what the five-talent person did. Notice what happens to this one-talent servant: What he most dreaded—losing his one talent—is exactly what happens to him. Because he did not use it profitably, it is taken away from him and given to a servant who will use it. Burying and hiding a talent will never preserve or save it. Rather, we can be sure we will lose our talents if we do not use them profitably.

If you find yourself in the working world, for whatever reason, and you are not motivated to go to greater heights in your career, ask yourself if you are using the talents given you to their fullest. Could it be laziness that is keeping you from pushing ahead? Are you squandering abilities that could be used? Remember too that God expects us to do our work with the highest possible excellence.

On the other hand, you may have ambitions that are not related to the working world. Your talents and ambitions may be more geared to other types of service. The world may never recognize that as success, but remember they don't keep God's books. If you are using your talent as God would have it be used, whether it furthers your career or not, then you are being a good and faithful servant.

So, is it all right not to be ambitious for promotions and titles and places of prominence in the working world? Absolutely. As long as you are certain that you are using your talents to your greatest ability, not hiding them or saving them. As long as you continually bring your priorities before God, and keep them in line with His purposes for your life.

Invisible Eyesight

One of my constant prayers is that God will give me "invisible eyesight." What is invisible eyesight? Paul said in 2 Corinthians 4:18 (PHILLIPS) that "We are looking all the time not at the visible things but at the invisible. The visible things are transitory: it is the invisible things that are really permanent." Invisible eyesight is the ability to see the things that are really permanent, though they are not seen by human eyes. I pray for invisible eyesight, so that I can see those invisible things. I do not want to be consumed with things that are transitory—things that exist for a short time only.

If you earnestly and sincerely ask God to give you invisible eyesight, this question of whether or not to be ambitious will be answered. As you see things from His perspective, your priorities will begin to change to His priorities.

A spiritually intelligent person, man or woman, will see the value of placing life's ambitions and energy into things that are permanent.

We end this chapter right where we started, with Jesus' advice to us as found in Matthew 6:33:

> But seek first His kingdom and His righteousness; and all these things shall be added to you.

Those few words spoken by our Master are all we need to know how to put our priorities in order for a balanced view of ambition, success and money.

Chapter Four

What the Well-Dressed Christian Working Woman Wears

Women have always loved clothes. It just seems to be part of our natures. Those of us with daughters can easily recall how they develop a great interest in their clothes at a very early age. Ever try to get a four-year-old girl to wear a dress she didn't like? Very hard to do. Or, for a real challenge, try a 14-year-old. Absolutely impossible! We women form opinions about our clothes very early in life, and we treat clothes as more than just coverings for our body. To some extent our very identity seems to be wrapped up in the clothes we wear.

Have you ever thought about how much time you spend on your clothes? You have to shop for them, decide which ones to wear, clean them, mend them, and match them. I think you might be surprised to see how much of your life is concerned with your wardrobe. Preoccupation with clothes can easily become excessive.

Do Clothes Make the Woman?

For those of us in the working world, clothes take on added importance. We become even more image conscious, as we recognize that our clothes contribute much to the impressions we make on other people. Our society places increased emphasis on clothes for the career-oriented woman, telling us that "clothes make the woman," and that we should "dress for success."

What about Christian working women? Should we be concerned about the clothes that we wear? We know that clothes do not make a person. Lasting worth and purpose in life only come as we establish a vital relationship with Jesus Christ. We know that God does not look on outward appearances; He looks at our hearts and judges us by how we are dressed inwardly. We read in 1 Samuel 16:7: "But the Lord said to Samuel, 'Do not look at his appearance or at the height of his stature, because I have rejected him; for God sees not as man sees, for man looks at the outward appearance, but the Lord looks at the heart.' "

Do you think this means that we should ignore the impact and effect of clothes? Should we strive to overcome our natural desire to dress beautifully and look good, and instead dress in some different way as Christian women?

Getting Your Priorities in Line

I do not believe that we are told to ignore what we wear, or to try to "dress down" because we are Christians. First Peter 3:3, 4 gives some good insight here:

> And let not your adornment be external only—braiding the
> hair, and wearing gold jewelry, or putting on dresses; but let

it be the hidden person of the heart, with the imperishable
quality of a gentle and quiet spirit, which is precious in the
sight of God.

Peter is directing this specifically to women. It is interesting to note that women were as much concerned with clothes and looks then as they are now. Notice that Peter does not admonish them *not* to adorn the external. He is not forbidding them to try new hairstyles, or wear nice clothes and jewelry. What he is saying is, get your priorities in line.

I get the feeling that those ladies in Peter's day had the same problem many of us have when it comes to clothes. Our natural tendency to dress nicely can easily get out of line, and those clothes can begin to take an undue place of importance and priority in our lives and in our thinking. Though men are not exempt from this problem, women are more susceptible to this unbalanced view of clothes, and we must be very careful to avoid this pitfall.

We can easily fall prey to the idea that our clothes make us more important or of more value. Clothes can become substitutes for the really important things in our lives. When I first started my sales career, I became a "clothes horse." There's just no other term for it. I bought clothes to make me feel good; I bought clothes to pick me up when I was down; I bought clothes to impress people; I bought clothes to try to attract men; I bought clothes to bolster my own feelings of self-worth; I bought clothes to overcome my inferiority feelings about my looks. I collected lots of nice clothes for many wrong reasons.

I was looking to clothes to meet emotional needs. I'm sure you know, without my telling you, that it did not work. The emotional needs I was trying to meet through clothes were only met when, after many years, I truly relinquished control of my life to my Lord, and He began to change my emotions and desires, and He met those needs.

Gradually I noticed that my intense desire to buy new clothes began to subside. It was not a conscious decision on my part at first. It was simply that God was working in me and showing me His priorities for my life. And as I continued to get to know Him and focus my thinking on Him, I no longer looked to clothes to meet certain needs.

Don't misunderstand me. I have not turned against pretty clothes! I'm just as normal as blueberry pie, and you'll find me "Oohing and aahing" over nice clothes and pretty jewelry just like anyone else. (In fact, as I write this, I am planning to go shopping this very day for a new outfit for a special presentation I have to give.) I am still very vulnerable to the desire for clothes, and I think I will always have to work at keeping my priorities straight in this area.

I do sincerely believe it is important for Christians to be careful in their dress and in their appearance, so as not to bring any dishonor to the Lord. Sloppiness and dowdiness are never condoned in God's Word. Peter, remember, did not tell the ladies to forsake adorning themselves outwardly. Rather, he told them to be sure they understood that external adornment was not nearly as important as internal adornment.

I believe another benefit of paying appropriate attention and care to how we look and what we wear is that we become less self-conscious. I've discovered that when I leave the house in the morning feeling that my hair, my outfit, and my overall appearance is close to optimum, then I can forget myself and how I look for the rest of the day. But if, on the other hand, I face a day feeling that my dress is not proper, or my hair is not becoming, then all day long I am thinking about myself, running into the ladies' room to try to improve my appearance, fussing with my clothes—in other words, I'm self-absorbed. In that condition I cannot be very effective at reaching out to other people and being concerned about their lives, because I'm too much into myself. For me, that is an important reason to spend the time and effort necessary to look as good as I can.

As Christian women in the working world, I believe, it is important that we dress in good taste and in good fashion. Clothes do contribute to others' impressions of us, and we should not ignore that fact. Furthermore, God made us feminine, with certain natural feminine tendencies, and in proper context, He does not condemn us for enjoying pretty clothes and nice things.

First Timothy 6:17 gives another clear principle for us to follow as we consider what our attitude toward these temporary things should be: "Instruct those who are rich in this present world not to be conceited or to fix their hope on the uncertainty of riches, but on God, who richly supplies us with all things to enjoy."

God has given us all things to enjoy—that includes clothes. Our responsibility is to be certain that we do not fix our hope or our central focus on these uncertain earthly things.

Our Special Wardrobe

I believe it is clear from these Scriptures that we should concern ourselves with adorning the inner person far more than we do the outward person. There is a very special wardrobe for a Christian working woman—or any Christian, anywhere. We should spend far more time acquiring and wearing these "clothes" than any outward garments. This wardrobe will set us apart from other women and identify us as women who love and serve Jesus Christ.

The wardrobe that I am referring to is totally within our reach, looks wonderful on all of us, and assures us of being very well dressed. It is described in Colossians 3:12–15.

> *And so, as those who have been chosen of God, holy and beloved, put on a heart of compassion, kindness, humility, gentleness and patience; bearing with one another, and forgiving each other, whoever has a complaint against any one; just as the Lord forgave you, so also should you. And beyond all these things put on love, which is the perfect bond of unity. And let the peace of Christ rule in your hearts, to which indeed you were called in one body, and be thankful.*

These are the special garments intended by God for each of us to wear on that inner person, and as Christian working women, we have a unique opportunity to be lights in our working world by learning how to wear these beautiful clothes. Let's look more closely at these inner garments.

The Wardrobe Described

Compassion   The first garment is compassion, which can be described as a deep feeling of sharing the suffering of another. You know, it's not hard to find suffering people these days. There is mental, physical, and emotional suffering everywhere, and undoubtedly you have suffering people all around you where you work. Are you aware of their suffering? Do you care?

It seems to me that all too often I am quick to blame people and judge them without stopping to think of what they have endured, or why they are the way they are. That's especially easy to do on our jobs. We judge our fellow workers without really understanding their suffering.

Don't you think compassion would look good on your job? If you wear it, you won't be so quick to condemn or judge. You'll give people room to make mistakes. Your prayer list will get longer, because when we care about people, we pray for them. Do you pray for the people you work with? Start praying for them and watch how much more compassionate you feel toward them. Yes, indeed, we need to wear compassion on our jobs.

Kindness   Kindness is the second garment in the closet of a well-dressed Christian woman. Have we been too busy to wear any kindness lately? Do we put it on and off, depending on our mood, or who we're with? Sometimes we are least kind to the people nearest to us. We seem to forget that kindness is important on our jobs, with those people we work with every day. It seems we save our kind behavior for people we don't see very often, as though it were in short supply. God has plenty of it, so wear it to work every day. You'll look terrific!

Humility   Third in this special wardrobe is humility. Society often gives negative connotations to humility, as though it were an undesirable characteristic. It is often viewed as weakness or a "Milquetoast" personality. Rarely do we think of humility as a necessity for getting to the top in the business world.

But that's an incorrect assessment of true humility. The Bible defines humility as a lack of pride, and an awareness of who we are in comparison to who God is. God hates pride. It's at the top of the list of things that He hates. If your assessment of yourself is inflated, and you have a know-it-all attitude, you're not wearing humility, and you're missing an important outfit in your wardrobe.

Gentleness   And then we come to gentleness. I am always overwhelmed with the amazing gentleness of Jesus Christ. Oh, how we need to wear His gentleness to work every day! We need that gentle and quiet spirit which Peter tells us should be our adornment, and which is precious in the sight of God.

Are your words tough or harsh? Do you have a sharp tongue or hasty actions that pierce and hurt people before you realize what you're doing? Then you undoubtedly need to wear more gentleness. Gentle answers turn away anger, we are told in Proverbs 15:1, and a gentle spirit brings peace to chaotic situations. It is a precious garment, and everyone will love it on you!

Patience   The next garment we find in this wardrobe for the inner person is patience. Patience can be defined as the capacity to calmly endure. I have to chuckle as I write that, because if anything is the opposite of what I am, it is calm endurance. This is a really difficult garment for me to wear; it just never seems to fit—always a little too small.

And yet God put it on His list, and He didn't make any exceptions, not even for me. You know, I'm learning that God can make this garment fit me—or rather, make me fit this garment—if I am willing to let Him. I've asked Him to help me put on patience, and since I've started asking, He has put me into situations that have taught me how to be patient. I'm learning—it fits better now than it did a year ago. If I can wear patience, so can you.

Tolerance   The next garment is "bearing with one an-other"—or tolerance. Tolerance is that beautiful quality of allowing other people to be different from us, even different from what we think they should be, and loving them and appreciating them for what they are. If we wore tolerance to work every day, we wouldn't be upset when people don't do just what we think they should do. We'd allow them more room for error. We'd bend over backwards to under-stand where they're coming from, and to give them more time to grow and learn.

How often I expect others to track along with me—to march to the same tune that my band is playing. And God has to remind me that He deals with each of us individually. Just because He is teaching me one lesson doesn't mean that all my friends have to learn it simultaneously! Tolerance is the garment that allows us to "bear with" others, whatever their circumstances.

Forgiveness   The word itself is beautiful. And, oh, what a wonderful garment to have and to wear. It brings so much happiness to others when we're able to forgive. God tells us to forgive others as He has forgiven us. That's pretty powerful forgiveness, isn't it? Are you harboring an unfor-giving attitude in your heart toward someone? Even if you have been mistreated, you need to put on forgiveness. Even if you haven't been asked to forgive, you need to wear for-giveness. And even if you've forgiven someone for the same thing time and again, you need to keep forgiving.

You'll be amazed to see that in forgiving others, you re-

lieve yourself of an immense burden of bitterness and resentment. And you experience God's forgiveness for you in
greater measure, so you rid yourself of guilt you've been
carrying around. Forgiveness for others reaps enormous
benefits for you. Put on forgiveness; it is lovely.

Peace is the next beautiful garment in God's wardrobe. Are you peaceful? Or do you fret and worry a lot? Is
your life frantic? Perfect peace comes by fixing your mind
on Jesus Christ. Have you tried any peace on lately? It is the
most wonderfully comfortable garment in the whole wardrobe. Once you try it on, you will want to wear it constantly.

Thankfulness is absolutely essential in your wardrobe if you want to be a well-dressed Christian working
woman. Do you complain a lot about what you don't have
or can't do or where you are or who you are? There usually
is lots of complaining going on in most any job environment. Are you a part of that complaining? If you wear
thankfulness, you won't complain. You'll be too busy
counting your blessings. Thankfulness is very attractive.
When you wear it you have a certain magnetism; people
love to be with you. It makes you a positive person and it
cures depression.

Have you been wearing thankfulness to work? It is a mag-
ical garment, because as we learn to give thanks in every situation, we discover that our heaviest burdens grow light
and easy.

Love And then as the crowning touch to all the other
garments in this unique wardrobe, we need to wear love.
Love is the golden chain of all these virtues. It is the finishing touch that brings the whole wardrobe together and
blends every garment into a unified appearance.

Love covers up blemishes; it fills in the missing gaps and mends the frayed edges. God's love, worn in our hearts, motivates us to want to wear all these garments.

So, here it is, God's wardrobe all ready for you to put on: compassion, kindness, humility, gentleness, patience, tolerance, forgiveness, peace, thankfulness, and love. You've heard it said that clothes make the person. Well, whether or not that's true with our outward clothes, it certainly is true with this special wardrobe for our inner person.

This wardrobe is totally within your reach, you can afford it, it will look absolutely marvelous on you, and will assure you of being a success in your Christian walk. If you wear this wardrobe on your job every day, you can be certain that you will be the best-dressed woman on the job!

But how in the world do we accomplish this? It's not difficult to talk about these garments, and it's easy for me to admonish you to wear them. But if you're finding that they just don't fit, or you don't know how in your everyday situation to be patient or kind or gentle or thankful, then how do you change? How can you put on these beautiful clothes that every Christian working woman should wear?

The Wardrobe Is Worn by Faith

The first thing we must understand is that putting on these garments is not an act of our emotions, it is an act of our will. So often in our Christian walk we want all the feelings in place before we exercise faith. We want to *feel* gentle and humble and peaceful and thankful. And if our feelings aren't working too well on a particular day, then we assume we just can't wear those garments that day, because we don't *feel* them. The sooner we learn that feelings cannot be trusted and cannot be used to measure our spiritual temperature, the sooner we'll be able to take these garments, *by faith*, and wear them.

When you know you're facing a day that will require, for instance, a great deal of patience, keep repeating that you *will* put on patience for that day. Put it on by faith, regardless of whether you feel patient or not. Your feelings will eventually give up and come along with your will, so never mind them. *Will* to do His will. God will supply the patience when you need it, if you don't allow your emotions to destroy your faith.

You wear these garments *by faith*, just as you accepted God's gift of eternal life *by faith*. The act of your *will* is your part; God does the rest.

The Wardrobe Is Not Personality Dependent

Second, wearing this wardrobe is not a function of our personalities. Many of these inner garments do not come naturally to our various personalities. But that does not keep any of us from wearing all of them.

I think that we often let ourselves off the hook by saying, "Well, that's just the way I am. I can't be anyone else; I have to be myself." We've been fed this current philosophy of "being your own person" so much, that we use it to excuse ourselves from whatever we feel doesn't "fit" our personalities.

Well, I can't see where God makes any exceptions for personality. He has all these garments you can ever need, and He's ready to impart them to you. Don't let your personality be an excuse for not making God's Best-Dressed

List. It is possible—through Christ—for all of us to wear this entire wardrobe.

This Wardrobe Needs an Uncluttered Closet

Maybe one reason you haven't put on all of these garments is that there just is not room in your "closet." Perhaps your wardrobe is cluttered with all kinds of outdated, ugly clothes. In the same third chapter of Colossians we have a list of clothes that we should "put off":

Anger   Anger is a legitimate reaction to unfair treatment, injustice, and so forth. But if we harbor anger instead of dealing with it properly, then it becomes a part of our wardrobe, and that's when anger becomes a sin. Regardless of whether our anger is justified or not, God tells us to put off anger. It is so unbecoming that if we took a look in the mirror and saw just how that anger looks on us, we'd shed it right away.

Wrath   Wrath is anger with resentment. Resentment is a beastly garment. It distorts our thinking, takes over our mind, and keeps us in a state of constant upset. Are you resentful *and* angry toward someone? You may not realize it, but others can see that wrath you are wearing, and it really is the wrong style for you.

Malice   Malice is the desire to see others suffer—spitefulness. It is uglier even than anger or wrath. When we hope that misfortune comes to someone who has made our life tough or unpleasant, that is malice. When we wish our boss would get fired, that is malice. And the world sees that malice we wear. It really is overpowering, and most unattractive.

Slander, abusive speech, and lying   These all go together as they are concerned with what comes out of our mouths. James was really on target when he talked about the tongue as a little flame which can kindle a great fire (*see* James 3:5). There is no place in God's wardrobe for this sort of speech coming from our mouths.

Are there any of these ugly clothes in your closet? They take up so much room and occupy so much of our time and thoughts that we're left with little room for the beautiful clothes that we need to wear. Sometimes we wear these unattractive clothes so long, that we begin to feel rather comfortable with them. But until we take them off, we won't know how heavy and confining and unbecoming they really are. They do not look good on anyone, not even once in a while.

Exchanging Our Ugly Wardrobe

In Isaiah 61, God says He will give us beauty for ashes, joy for mourning, and a garment of praise for the spirit of heaviness. What an incredible offer this is from our Heavenly Father! He wants to exchange all those heavy, ugly, dirty clothes now hanging in our personality wardrobe, and in return give us beauty and joy and a garment of praise.

I ask you, in all reasonableness, *How could any straight-thinking woman refuse His offer?* The only thing required is that we be willing to exchange our present unsightly wardrobe for His new garments. We must relinquish the control of our life to the Heavenly Father, and be willing to take off our present unattractive clothes, hand them over to Him, and accept in exchange the beautiful inner garments that He desires to give us.

A Special Closet

If we're going to possess these special clothes, we must prepare a special place for them. It is the closet of prayer, to which Jesus referred when He was teaching His disciples how to pray.

We wear these garments in direct proportion to the quality of our prayer life. Without a "prayer closet," we'll find these garments very difficult to keep. And that prayer closet includes God talking to us through His Word, as well as our petitions to Him.

I ask you, how much time did you spend today praying and meditating on God's Word? Yesterday? This week? Did other less significant, optional activities, such as television or reading the paper or magazines, occupy more of your time than prayer?

God is showing me that if I really am serious about being His woman all the way, as I say I am, my prayer life must be consistent and strong and must occupy the most important place in my priorities as I schedule my time every day. A prayer closet is essential for the preservation of this heavenly wardrobe!

This Wardrobe Should Be Worn Daily

If you really want to be a well-dressed Christian working woman, and wear all of these clothes at once (you won't be overdressed!), I have a suggestion to help you. Every morning as you get dressed, as you put on your underwear and hose, blouse and skirt, your jacket and coat, talk to the Lord, saying something like this: "Lord, while I'm putting on these necessary outer garments, I want You to know that I desire to be Your best-dressed woman. I want to put on compassion, kindness, humility, gentleness, patience, peace, thankfulness, tolerance, and love."

Make a list and tack it on your closet door as a reminder. Memorize the list. And repeat to God every day, using your dressing time as a reminder, that you desire to wear these beautiful clothes He has provided. And *by faith*, as you put on your outer garments, you are at the same time putting on these inner clothes.

One of Satan's best methods for defeating us is forgetfulness. He'll try to erase your memory and keep you from thinking about God's inner wardrobe. If you don't find a method to remind yourself, you'll be surprised at how other things will crowd your mind, and the day will be over before you've remembered what you should be wearing. You'll find that you've gone the whole day without the proper clothes. This little routine will help you remember.

Recently, a friend of mine took my advice and literally taped this list of inner garments to her mirror. She told me that it was a great help to her in reminding her daily as she dressed, of the most important clothes she should be putting on. Why don't you try it on your mirror? See if it helps.

Looking in God's Mirror

In James 1:23–26, we read that a person who simply hears and does nothing about what she hears is like a woman catching the reflection of her own face in a mirror. She sees herself, it is true, but she goes on with whatever she was doing, without the slightest recollection of what sort of person she saw in the mirror.

After we dress each day, the last thing we do is check the mirror. To look in the mirror and discover a serious problem with our clothes, and then do nothing about the problem is rather ridiculous. The whole purpose of looking into the mirror is to remedy any problem before we go out to face the world.

Have you looked into the mirror lately? What have you been wearing? Do you need a new wardrobe? Are you tired of the drab, weary, heavy clothes in your closet? Don't walk away from God's mirror without doing something about what you saw. The Bible tells us that to those who know to do good and do it not, to them it is sin.

What happens when you start to take seriously this idea of putting on God's beautiful clothes on a daily basis? A couple of years ago, as I struggled with lack of patience and kindness and gentleness in my life, I began practicing this principle daily and I continue doing it to this very day, consciously putting on patience and kindness and gentleness, along with the other garments.

Then I began to realize what happened. I was keenly aware of my lack of these things during the day. That's the first step. As soon as I would be unkind, my spirit would convict me. God's voice inside me would say, "Kindness just fell off, Mary. Put it back on, please." Then I gradually became aware that I was handling situations and people with more compassion than before. I discovered I really cared about other people's feelings, and I *wanted* to be kind and gentle. My speech became more tolerant and kind. And to my utter amazement, I discovered that I was becoming patient in situations where before I would have been impossible.

Oh, there is much room left for improvement, but I can testify that it works to put on God's wardrobe every day. And when you go to your job wearing these clothes, you're going to stand out as the best-dressed woman in your working environment. Everyone loves compassion and kindness, gentleness and love, thankfulness and tolerance. They're always in style.

This is not meant to be just a clever way of talking about the fruits of God's Spirit. Rather it is meant to be a practical way to help you put on these lovely inner garments and watch God transform your life. I challenge you to wear these clothes, by faith, every day, and become the best-dressed woman on the job.

Chapter Five

Feminine Assertiveness

Assertiveness—even aggressiveness—on the job is quite acceptable for men. Indeed, it is expected and admired. But are the rules the same for the women who are now part of the business scene—who are holding positions that until recently were available only to men? Can a woman be effectively assertive in the business world?

The Christian woman has an even tougher issue to confront: Is feminine assertiveness compatible with Christian principles? We've just been talking about a wardrobe of gentleness, humility, and patience. How does assertiveness fit in with these garments?

There is a general attitude in some Christian circles that it is never appropriate for a woman to be assertive. Some would lay guilt trips on women who aspire to hold positions that require strong leadership, as though no truly "spiritual" woman would have such aims. Many Christian working women are understandably confused about this matter of asserting themselves on their jobs. What is appropriate? What isn't?

Assertiveness vs. Aggressiveness

In a moment we'll take a look at biblical guidelines as they apply to feminine assertiveness. But first, let's clarify our terms. *Assertive* and *aggressive* are often confused. Sometimes they are used interchangeably, while at other times they are used to contrast acceptable and nonacceptable behavior.

Aggressive is usually an acceptable attribute for a man but quite unacceptable for a woman. To say that a man is aggressive is not necessarily a negative description, while the label of aggressive for a woman generates visions of a "pushy broad" whose behavior is unfeminine and undesirable. *Assertive* is usually a more acceptable label, whether used for men or women. Unquestionably, double standards still exist when comparing male and female behavior in business.

For our purposes here we will use dictionary definitions. *Assertiveness* is characterized by confidence, positiveness, and firmly stating and defending one's rights and opinions.

Aggressiveness, on the other hand, has a much more negative definition. It is characterized by hostile attacks and forcefulness. It is selfish action that does not take into consideration the good of others, only one's own gain and advancement, frequently at the expense of other people and their rights.

With this differentiation between assertiveness and aggressiveness, we can easily see that aggressive action is inappropriate for any Christian, because it does not bear any of the marks of the fruits of the Holy Spirit, particularly, kindness, gentleness, love, or peace.

Our discussion will focus then, on assertiveness, which

can be characterized as confident, affirmative, bold, and firm behavior, which is frequently required in leadership roles and often necessary in accomplishing goals and tasks. Some personalities are more naturally assertive than others. But whether or not it comes naturally to us, we need to know how and when we can and should be assertive, particularly as Christian working women facing new roles and circumstances.

Biblical Role Models

Let's start by looking at some women in the Bible to see what we can learn about assertiveness from them. There are many examples, but we will look only at four.

Deborah

First is Deborah, who was a judge over her whole nation, the top ruler in Israel for many years. Talk about a lady ahead of her time—Deborah would be considered very assertive in *today's* society. Imagine how unique she must have been in her own day, when women's roles were much more limited.

God chose her at that point in history to deliver His people from a foreign oppressor. The details of her story are found in Judges 3 and 4. As a judge she undoubtedly was required to demonstrate assertive leadership on a day-to-day basis, but at one point she demonstrated *unusual* assertiveness—as she led her army into battle:

> *Now she [Deborah] sent and summoned Barak the son of Abinoam from Kedesh-naphtali, and said to him, "Behold, the Lord, the God of Israel, has commanded, 'Go and march*

to Mount Tabor, and take with you ten thousand men from the sons of Naphtali and from the sons of Zebulun. And I will draw out to you Sisera, the commander of Jabin's army, with his chariots and his many troops to the river Kishon; and I will give him into your hand.' " Then Barak said to her, "If you will go with me, then I will go; but if you will not go with me, I will not go." And she said, "I will surely go with you; nevertheless, the honor shall not be yours on the journey that you are about to take, for the Lord will sell Sisera into the hands of a woman." Then Deborah arose and went with Barak to Kedesh. And Barak called Zebulun and Naphtali together to Kedesh, and ten thousand men went up with him; Deborah also went up with him.

And Deborah said to Barak, "Arise! For this is the day in which the Lord has given Sisera into your hands; behold, the Lord has gone out before you." So Barak went down from Mount Tabor with ten thousand men following him. And the Lord routed Sisera and all his chariots and all his army, with the edge of the sword before Barak; and Sisera alighted from his chariot and fled away on foot. But Barak pursued the chariots and the army as far as Harosheth-hagoyim, and all the army of Sisera fell by the edge of the sword; not even one was left.

Judges 4:6–10; 14–16

Deborah led her army into a battle that was absolutely doomed for failure by all the evidence. But she asked God for a miracle, and He delivered her people from the hands of their overwhelming enemy.

This most unusual assignment for a woman—to lead an army—required a great deal of assertiveness. Deborah was chosen by God for this leadership role, and she was effectively assertive as a leader. This was part of God's plan. Deborah did not rise to this position by accident. She didn't run for election as our leaders do. She was appointed by God, and she was assertive in a very unusual way.

Esther

Then there is Esther, who delivered her people, but remained within a traditional role to do so. She became the queen and used that position to prevent her people from being annihilated. Assertive—yes. But in a different way from Deborah. Her assertiveness was much less obvious, yet nonetheless courageous and effective.

A passage from the book of Esther gives us an insight into this incredible woman.

> Then Esther spoke to Hathach and ordered him to reply to Mordecai: "All the king's servants and the people of the king's provinces know that for any man or woman who comes to the king to the inner court who is not summoned, he has but one law, that he be put to death, unless the king holds out to him the golden scepter so that he may live. And I have not been summoned to come to the king for these thirty days." And they related Esther's words to Mordecai.

> Then Mordecai told them to reply to Esther, "Do not imagine that you in the king's palace can escape any more than all the Jews. For if you remain silent at this time, relief and deliverance will arise for the Jews from another place and you and your father's house will perish. And who knows whether you have not attained royalty for such a time as this?"

Then Esther told them to reply to Mordecai, "Go, assemble all the Jews who are found in Susa, and fast for me; do not eat or drink for three days, night or day. I and my maidens also will fast in the same way. And thus I will go in to the king, which is not according to the law; and if I perish, I perish."

So Mordecai went away and did just as Esther had commanded him.

Esther 4:10–17

Esther was the one person who could approach the king and attempt to save her people, the Jews, from the annihilation planned by their enemy, Haman. Esther well knew that unless the king intervened, a person approaching his presence without his permission would automatically be put to death. But she made her plans, and without regard for her own life, she approached the king with her plan. Through this assertive action she saved her people.

The Proverbs Woman

Then there is the woman described in Proverbs 31. No woman could accomplish all she did without being assertive. Her major role was mother and wife, and she never lost sight of that priority. She was a hardworking woman who managed her household of many servants. In addition she had a real estate business and a manufacturing business, making and selling linen garments and belts.

Sometimes when I think I have a lot to do, I read Proverbs 31. The exceptional woman described there has many roles to fulfill, and she does so with excellence. You can sense her confidence and firm leadership as she performs her many duties.

Being assertive did not conflict with her family duties or ruin her testimony. Her children called her blessed and she was a joy to her husband. She used the talents and abilities God gave her to their fullest.

Lydia

Lydia is a New Testament example of an assertive lady. She was a seller of purple fabrics, which was a prestigious occupation. It is obvious from her profession and the description of her home that Lydia had achieved considerable success in her business. Through the Apostle Paul she comes into a personal knowledge of Jesus Christ, and afterward her home becomes the headquarters for Paul while he is in Philippi.

She brought her whole household to a knowledge of Jesus as Savior, and through her home and her resources the Gospel spread to Europe. This was an assertive woman, exhibiting leadership and firm convictions, using what God had given her to be what He wanted her to be. Her story is found in Acts 16.

Guidelines for Assertiveness

What I learn from these women in Scripture is that assertiveness—that confident, positive leadership and ingenuity they demonstrated—is acceptable and commendable for

God's women. All of these women were admirable,
respected women, operating with God's approval and
blessing.

Feminine Guidelines

One thing is obvious about these four women in the
Bible: They were effectively assertive without losing or
abandoning their femininity. Even when they operated in
nontraditional roles, they never forgot that they were
women, and their assertiveness was within the context of
their femininity.

Like me, you have probably witnessed many women in
today's environment who thought that to be effectively assertive, they needed to pattern their behavior after their
male peers. Whatever the measure of their success, it is my
experience and belief that they would have been more successful had they not left their natural feminine characteris-
tics behind as they asserted themselves. God made each sex
unique, with different strengths to complement the other.
When we try to eliminate those God-designed differences,
we put ourselves at a disadvantage and lose a great deal of
our effectiveness.

A natural question would then be, What is feminine and
what is not? It would be rather neat and clean if it were
possible to give a definitive list that worked in every situation. If I dared to define feminine assertiveness in terms of
specifics, unquestionably I would be challenged on each
one. Much of the determination is instinctive, and what
would or would not be feminine for me would not hold true
for all women. The guidelines on the next few pages are

presented to help in your own determination of what is or is not within the context of your feminine personality.

Circumstantial and Personality Guidelines

It is important to notice that these examples of assertive women in the Bible show a variety of styles. There is no one role model for assertiveness for women, no one single, rigid guideline that every woman has to follow. Each of them had a style and degree of assertiveness in harmony with her circumstances and personality.

Of the four, Deborah was the most assertive, but her circumstances demanded unusually strong leadership. Esther was required to be ingenious and shrewd in asserting herself. Had she approached the king with a strong verbal style of assertiveness, it could have meant her own death, as well as the annihilation of her people. The Proverbs woman demonstrated a quiet kind of leadership and assertiveness, gently but firmly performing her duties with skill and excellence. Lydia achieved a place of prominence by asserting herself in her business, and then she used that God-given ability to help spread the Gospel to people who had never heard.

Our assertiveness should also be measured by the context of our circumstances and personalities. We must carefully assess the situations we face and determine what degree of assertiveness is called for and will be effective. To begin with, we must be well aware of our own personalities and what style is appropriate for us.

I remember one particular situation when I was assertive for the right reason, but at the wrong time, in the wrong way, and out of character with my own personality. I was in a meeting with my peers and my manager, discussing a proposed change in procedures for my department. I came totally prepared to explain why my proposal was superior to the one currently being considered, which was my manager's idea. I presented my reasons in a very reasonable, documented fashion, not expecting to find any resistance, for it was fairly obvious—at least to me—that this was the best course for the company.

For reasons unknown to me, my proposal struck at a very raw nerve and my manager was furious. While he could not deny that my reasoning was correct, he was very angry that I was opposing his suggestion. My peers stated their opinion that my method was the better of the two, and so very grudgingly the decision was made to accept my proposal.

However, in making the concession certain remarks and accusations were made. Mind you, the remarks were inaccurate and unfair. They were angry words spoken out of turn, and I should have let them go unanswered. Nothing could be gained under the circumstances by any further protestations on my part. But in retributive anger, I made my opposition known in strong terms, which, of course, just made matters worse.

The circumstances did not call for further assertiveness on my part. Furthermore, I have never been particularly effective at retorts and confrontations, especially when they take me by surprise. If I had been quiet at that point, later on I might have had an opportunity to object effectively to the unfair accusations. Certainly my Christian testimony would have been strengthened, for my restrained behavior would have stood in stark contrast to the unrestrained behavior of my manager. I failed to follow the guidelines of keeping within the context of the circumstances and my own personality.

So, it is very important that we are assertive when it is appropriate and can be effective. But it is equally important that we learn to use assertiveness sparingly and in balance with the circumstances and our personalities.

A really good rule of thumb is "When in doubt, don't!" If you have a desire to assert yourself or your ideas in a given situation, but you are unsure if it's the right time or the right place, wait. If assertiveness is appropriate, it will most likely be just as effective tomorrow as today. Waiting will rarely be a wrong course when you are hesitant about the appropriateness of being assertive.

On the other hand, don't hold back for lack of courage when you are convinced that something must be said or done. If it is the right time and the right place, gird up your courage and do what you think is appropriate.

Biblical Guidelines

The most important things we Christian working women need to know are the Bible principles that apply to assertiveness. Our guidelines are not necessarily the accepted standards of the day. We are not governed by current mores or pervading attitudes. Our priority is to know what pleases the Lord. We need to be guided and motivated by obedience to the Word of God without hesitation and without questioning.

As I've faced various situations in my career, I've discovered some wonderful guidelines in Scripture to show me how to behave, how assertive to be, and what form that assertiveness should take. I am convinced that none of us will ever encounter a situation that will not fall under a biblical guideline if we truly desire to know what that guideline is. Let me share some of those specific passages that have been of great help to me in this question of assertiveness.

> But the wisdom from above is first pure, then peaceable, gentle, reasonable, full of mercy and good fruits, unwavering, without hypocrisy.
>
> James 3:17

Many times, when facing a decision as to whether or not it was appropriate for me to assert my own ideas, I have used this verse as a testing station. If the wisdom is from God, our motives will be pure, there will be a continuing peace about the situation, our emotions will be under control and therefore gentle, our thinking will be reasonable, and the objectives of our assertive behavior will be for the good of others as well as ourselves. If our proposed action does not pass this fairly stringent test, then it is questionable.

If, however, it does pass this test, we need to act. Remember that even though we believe our proposed action meets these requirements, it may still be a tough thing for us to do. Just because we have a certain amount of apprehension about being assertive does not necessarily signal that it is not God's peaceable wisdom.

There have been times when I've made a decision to take a firm stand on some issue and to assert my own ideas. Yet when that moment comes, there are butterflies in my stomach and the palms of my hands are wet with perspiration. Depending on the significance of the action, and depending on your experience in being assertive, you may also encounter this nervousness at similar moments. That is not necessarily a sign that you don't have God's peace in the matter. His peace is that inner conviction that it is the right thing to do, and if you have that conviction and your idea passes the other tests as well, you don't have to be overly concerned about that natural nervousness.

Let's look at a few passages from Proverbs:

> *The wise in heart will be called discerning, And sweetness of speech increases persuasiveness.*
>
> Proverbs 16:21

The purpose of assertiveness, in many cases, is to be persuasive. We often need to be persuasive in business. But how do we do that? The Bible says that "sweetness of speech increases persuasiveness." Does that sound like a principle you would learn in today's MBA courses? It's rather opposite to "winning through intimidation," or many of the other ways of being persuasive that are promoted today.

I remember when the Lord first gave me this verse for a particular situation on my job. I felt as though I was being "run over" a bit. As a matter of fact, I was. My suggestions and ideas were more or less dismissed as unimportant. I felt that because I was the only female on the management team, there was an atmosphere of humoring me and tolerating me, but never taking me seriously.

I kept trying to change the situation by being more forceful. I'm sure my ruffled feathers frequently showed as I argued my positions and tried to get my ideas accepted. Before I realized it, I had assumed an adversary role, and I was getting nowhere. My powers of persuasion became less and less effective.

Then I came across this verse one morning in my quiet

time with the Lord. "Sweetness of speech increases persuasiveness." Could that be true in this situation? As I medi-
tated on this verse, I realized that *sweetness* here does not
mean gushy or coy or emotional, but rather, easy to swallow. It is analogous to the way we sugar-coat medicine so
children will take it. Sweetness makes things palatable.

I realized that indeed this verse gave me an important
guideline to use in my predicament. I gave it thought and
prayer, and asked God for wisdom in applying this principle. As soon as I stopped concentrating on the condescend-
ing treatment that I felt I was receiving, and concentrated
instead on finding ways to make my ideas palatable, I
started to win. I became more persuasive. By coating my
speech and considering the effect of my words, I began little by little to assert my own ideas effectively. Then I was
taken more seriously and gradually earned my rightful
place as a part of the team, no longer an outsider.

This is basic psychology that works in any relationship.
Try it with your husband or your children, the people who
report to you, or your colleagues at work. Discover how
sweetness of speech can increase your persuasiveness and
make you effectively assertive.

Let's look at another verse.

> By forbearance a ruler may be persuaded, And a soft tongue
> breaks the bone.
>
> *Proverbs 25:15*

Forbearance means tolerance and restraint in the face of
provocation. This verse says a ruler—a manager, a boss—
can be persuaded through tolerance and restraint.

Would you like to change your manager's mind about

something? Are you running into a brick wall? Forbear, be tolerant and restrained, and have a soft tongue, a gentle tongue, even in the face of provocation. Certainly, being able to persuade one's boss is effective assertiveness, and this verse gives a clear guideline on how to be persuasive with those in authority. It may take a little longer than you would like, but this approach will be successful.

Martha worked for a truly unreasonable manager. She never seemed to be able to get to first base, when it came to asserting her ideas. For over two years, while she was praying about the situation and trying to apply this principle of forbearance and tolerance, there seemed to be no evidence that she was making any headway whatsoever with her boss.

However, after this long period of seeing no results, in a meeting with her boss, he told her that he had great respect and admiration for her, and expressed a desire that he could be more like her. It really took her by surprise, because she had not been able to see that her tolerance in the situation was having any effect whatsoever. But this manager was testing her and watching her all that time, and he admitted that her behavior and life-style had made an indelible impression on him.

God has a right to use situations like this in our lives to bring glory to His name, and we may not even be aware that He is doing it. Forbearance is waiting on the Lord, patiently giving Him time to accomplish His purposes.

Pride goes before destruction, And a haughty spirit before stumbling.

Proverbs 16:18

Assertiveness, out of control, can easily take on a know-it-all attitude with an arrogant and haughty spirit. Often a little success will go to our heads. When we have been effectively assertive in one instance, we start to think that we have the tiger by the tail and we take on a prideful and haughty attitude. When this happens you can be sure of one thing: Stumbling and failure are right around the corner. Pride is a hideous sin, which plagues us most when we have had a measure of success. I often remind myself that pride is at the top of the list of the things God hates most. We must carefully monitor our thoughts and our attitudes to be sure that pride in our accomplishments does not creep in.

These are a few of the many verses that give us guidelines in assertiveness to apply to our jobs. They are God's principles of behavior, and they hold true for all Christians, male or female. They are God's psychology, and since He is the Creator, He understands how to deal with human nature better than anyone else.

Our responsibility remains very simple, though not always easy, and that is to obey without hesitation. Jesus said that those who love Him keep His commandments. Our obedience is the measure of our love for Him.

Just because these principles are not compatible with most of today's accepted rules does not mean that they are not effective. This world has not outgrown God's principles. It is true that God's methods will often be at variance with the world's. But we will find as we apply them that they really work, while the world's methods lead us to sure defeat.

Perhaps you are asking, "Then how do we account for all the successful people in the business world who are not

Christians?" Well, some of them do follow God's principles, and even though they are not consciously serving God, God still honors His principles. There are many honest, moral people who will enjoy God's blessing on their efforts because of their commitment to right thinking and acting.

Second, when we speak of success we must think long-term. It is possible to win through intimidation, to be dishonest and come out ahead, to climb the ladder on the backs of other people, to play political games and gain promotions thereby, to compromise moral standards and have temporary success. People do it all the time.

But in the winning they create many enemies and problems that come back to haunt them later on. What you sow you reap; it is a basic principle that cannot be escaped. We may not always be around for the harvest, to see the end result. It may be eternity before some people reap what they have sown, both good and bad. But you can be absolutely certain that harvesttime will come.

What I have noticed is that more often than not people who disregard God's principles have very short-term success. And even that success brings them no peace or satisfaction.

God's ways are peaceable, we can live with them easily. They won't keep us awake at night wondering how to cover our tracks.

A Gentle and Quiet Spirit

Before concluding this subject of assertiveness, there is one Scripture reference which often comes up when we speak of women's behavior. It should be addressed here.

In the same way, you wives, be submissive to your own hus-
bands so that even if any of them are disobedient to the
word, they may be won without a word by the behavior of
their wives, as they observe your chaste and respectful be-
havior. And let not your adornment be external only—
braiding the hair, and wearing gold jewelry, and putting on
dresses; but let it be the hidden person of the heart, with the
imperishable quality of a gentle and quiet spirit, which is
precious in the sight of God.

1 Peter 3:1–4

Frequently this passage is confusing to women, particularly women in leadership roles. Maybe you, too, have
wondered if this passage means that women are to be seen
and not heard. Does the gentle and quiet spirit spoken of
here prevent us from being assertive?

This passage is directed to wives, particularly those who
are married to unbelievers. Peter gives them a principle for
winning their husbands to Christ. It is a principle that works
in any close relationship when an unbeliever is united to a
believer.

What is it about a Christian that is inviting to a non-
Christian? Is it a constant barrage of words and Bible verses
and condemnation and judgment? Obviously not. That kind
of behavior doesn't attract anyone to anything.

But if we are especially close to a non-Christian—say a
husband, a brother or sister, a parent, even a roommate or a
very close friend—we can easily become lecturers and
judges and critics. I think Peter's message has a much
broader meaning for us, which is, if we are trying to win
someone to Jesus Christ, someone who is very close to us,

the best thing we can do is let them see in our lives that Christianity works. Peter says that "without a word" they may be won.

Our Lord's Assertiveness

Peter tells us that a quiet and gentle spirit is precious in the sight of God. This kind of attitude is not intended to be limited to women only. We know that because the same words were used by our Lord to describe His own spirit:

> Come to Me, all who are weary and heavy-laden, and I will give you rest. Take My yoke upon you, and learn from Me, for I am gentle and humble in heart; and you shall find rest for your souls. For My yoke is easy, and My load is light (emphasis added).
>
> Matthew 11:28–30

We can easily understand why this gentle spirit is so precious to God, since it was the spirit of His beloved Son. Women, as well as men, need to have a gentle and quiet spirit.

Frequently Jesus treated people with gentleness and compassion when others were condemning and intolerant. For example, the woman taken in adultery, the Samaritan woman He found at the well, Zacchaeus the hated tax collector, the blind man who wouldn't be silenced until Jesus healed him, the woman who touched His garment, the hungry crowds who had come to hear Him teach—the list is endless.

Then at His trial, Jesus did something we would never expect, in refusing to defend Himself against all false accusations. Every time I read those passages in John 18 and 19 and Matthew 27, I want to cry out, "Lord, don't let them say those things about You. Don't let them accuse You falsely. Defend Yourself!" But Jesus knew that this was His destiny; it was necessary, and it was His Father's will, so He refused to demand His rights, and instead never uttered a word.

His silence, however, was not an indication of weakness. He was in no way intimidated by His accusers. His not openly asserting Himself in this instance was a result of His choice to do the Father's will. He had settled that issue the night before in Gethsemane, when in agony He affirmed to His Father, "Not My will, but Thine, be done" (Luke 22:42).

Verbal assertiveness is not the only avenue through which we can be strong. In fact, it is often the easy way out for us. Gentleness is much more demanding and requires greater discipline and self-control. In most cases, gentleness will get us further than a verbal, outwardly assertive attitude. Remember, gentleness is not weak; rather, it is strength under control.

A gentle and quiet spirit does not, however, prevent us from being assertive. Jesus was frequently bold and assertive in His words and in His actions. Think of how He threw the money changers out of the temple, when they were misusing God's house for their own personal gain. Without hesitation He asserted His authority and literally ran them out quite unceremoniously. (*See* Matthew 21:12,13.)

The Gospels tell us of many of His confrontations with the religious hypocrites of His day. He wasted no words in condemning them and telling them in no uncertain terms just what He thought about them. Matthew 23 reveals His strong words to the scribes and the Pharisees. He pronounces judgment on them, calls them hypocrites, blind guides, fools, sons of murderers, and serpents. No Milquetoast, this Man. No weak, spineless philosopher/teacher.

His gentle and quiet spirit was appropriately assertive when the circumstances called for it, and that assertiveness was in keeping with His own personality.

Jesus is our supreme example for appropriate assertiveness. He had the perfect balance in His life and knew when to be vocal and take action and when to be silent.

The Right Motivation

An important characteristic of Jesus' assertiveness is that His motivation transcended His own individual rights. Though frequently falsely accused and maligned, He never defended Himself or His own reputation. He stood against evil and injustice; He condemned hypocrisy and evil. But never did He become assertive in defense of His own personal rights. Time and again He asserted His authority, but never strictly for His own personal gain.

When you think of the four women we cited earlier, you can say the same thing about them. Their assertiveness was never just on their own behalf. Certainly they benefited by their assertive actions. Deborah saved her people from being taken captive by Sisera, and in doing so she saved herself. Esther prevented the annihilation of the Jews, including herself. The Proverbs woman provided well for herself as well as for her household. While Lydia advanced the Gospel of Jesus Christ through the resources she had earned in her profession, she also enjoyed those resources herself.

It is not wrong to be assertive for a cause that will benefit

us. But if our only objective is to defend ourselves or demand our personal rights, without regard for the effect
on our testimony or on others, we are on very thin ice
spiritually.

Often assertiveness in the business world is used simply
to demand one's rights. People readily become aggressive
when they think their personal rights are being violated.

Recently I read an advice column in a secular magazine
for working women. It seems that a new manager had come
on the scene and changed all the rules for the particular
woman who had written for advice. Money and privileges
given her by her former boss were abruptly taken away and
promises broken. The advice given to her by a leading business consultant and job counselor consisted of two pages of
how to strike back at that company, how to outwit that
manager, how to get revenge for the wrong done to her,
how to cause legal problems for the parent company, and
how to take advantage of them to the fullest extent.

As I read this article, my natural tendency was to react,
"Right! Fight for what is yours and get your pound of
flesh." That is what our human nature will always lead us to
do, for we are born with self on the throne of our lives. But I
realized that if this lady follows the advice given, many
other people will suffer. It was apparent that customers
would suffer, other employees would suffer, and other managers would suffer. And there was no guarantee that by in-
flicting all this suffering, this woman would have achieved
anything at all for herself, except vengeance.

How often our drive to be assertive is totally motivated
by self-interest without regard for others. In other words,
remembering the definitions we gave earlier, it does not

take much for assertiveness to turn into aggressiveness. Our fallen, sinful nature just naturally rises up and demands that our territory be protected, our rights be held inviolable. But that is not the kind of assertiveness we see in Jesus.

The Guiding Principle

In summary, as Christians we have an overriding principle under which we operate. Our actions must always bring glory to God. There are times when assertiveness is totally compatible with that objective. As we have already seen, Jesus was frequently assertive in His actions and words. But there are times in our business lives when it will not be appropriate for us to be assertive, even if the cause is right. There are times when we must back away from defending our rights, and let God be our defense.

I am well aware of how difficult it is to let go of a situation where we feel our treatment is unjust, and to allow God to be our defense and settle the accounts. But if we could just practice that principle, and let God have a chance to prove how beautifully it works, we would be amazed to see that God's defense is far better than our own.

We're back to that underlying basic structure that is necessary for any of us who want to be what God wants us to be, and that is to yield our wills to His control. Giving up our rights. Giving up our right to be assertive, if that is what the situation calls for.

I fully understand that this does not correlate with society's current passion for standing up for your rights. And I am not saying that we should not take stands against injustice or prejudice or unfair treatment, whether it is directed toward us or toward others. But if our form of assertiveness is simply to fight for our own personal rights and our own personal gains, then it does not conform to the example given us by our Lord.

A good question to ask yourself is, would Jesus be assertive here? Remember, His kind of assertiveness was against evil and for the good of others. If we Christian working women could start to apply this principle on our jobs, our colleagues would soon have to take notice.

An assertiveness which is controlled by these principles is so different from what people expect, they will not be able to avoid the light they see in us. And the saltiness of our lives will make them thirsty.

And that's the bottom line: How can we be salt and light in this world where we work? That's what counts for eternity. Far more important than establishing new roles and blazing new frontiers for women is our directive to be witnesses in a dark and tasteless world.

If this sounds difficult or too idealistic to you, I would encourage you to rethink your reaction. It may be difficult, but it is so much easier than constantly standing vigil over your own rights and interests. And if it seems idealistic, it's only because so few Christians have ever dared to apply God's principles in the workplace, that we have few role models.

Why don't we break some new ground and determine to be assertive as Jesus would be? As one woman whose natural tendency is to fight hard for her own rights and for fair treatment, I can tell you that His way is so much better. It is peaceable and pure, and far more effective than the world's methods.

Chapter Six

~

Loving the People We Don't Like

Getting along with other people, whether they be family or friends, whether the relationship is of our choosing or one we cannot escape, whether it be a short- or long-term association, is always a challenge and seldom easy. But in learning to get along with other people, we can learn a great deal about ourselves—and grow in the process. Relationships are often God's sandpaper, which He uses to smooth the rough edges in our lives.

In the working world, we usually have little to say about who our co-workers will be. We find we are in the company of people who don't think as we do, who don't have the same values we do, who don't have similar life-styles to ours. They are people we would never choose as friends, yet in our jobs we are forced to spend many hours each week in close association with them. If we were candid, we would probably admit that we frequently work with people we do not really like. It is an environment ready-made for problems in getting along with others.

Liking or Loving

What can we do as Christians when we find ourselves in this kind of situation? How can we get along with people we don't like?

The first thing to understand is that running into people you don't like is unavoidable. There is no reason to feel guilty just because you do not like certain persons. It's okay! Admit it, you don't like them.

I'm sure there were people Jesus did not like. Read what He said to the religious hypocrites of His day:

> *You blind guides, who strain out a gnat and swallow a camel! Woe to you, scribes and Pharisees, hypocrites! For you clean the outside of the cup and of the dish, but inside they are full of robbery and self-indulgence. You blind Pharisee, first clean the inside of the cup and of the dish, so that the outside of it may become clean also. Woe to you, scribes and Pharisees, hypocrites! For you are like white-washed tombs which on the outside appear beautiful, but inside they are full of dead men's bones and all uncleanness. Even so you too outwardly appear righteous to men, but inwardly you are full of hypocrisy and lawlessness.*
>
> Matthew 23:24–28

And that's not all He said. The entire twenty-third chapter of Matthew is similar in tone. Frankly, I cannot imagine any stronger words against someone's character than these words of Jesus. Now, could you realistically say that Jesus liked these people? His feelings toward them do not seem to be those you have toward people you like. In my mind, it is obvious that Jesus did not like those scribes and Pharisees.

I think it is clear that even Christians are allowed to have people in their lives they do not like. I know of no scriptural directive which commands us to like everyone.

But I know many verses that tell us to *love* other people. Let me mention a few:

> *And this commandment we have from Him, that the one who loves God should love his brother also.*
>
> *1 John 4:21*

> *The one who does not love does not know God, for God is love.*
>
> *1 John 4:8*

> *[Jesus said] . . . Love your enemies. . . . if you love those who love you, what credit is that to you? For even sinners love those who love them.*
>
> *Luke 6:35, 32*

> *You shall love your neighbor as yourself.*
>
> *Leviticus 19:18*

These are just a few of the many verses that give us a clear directive to love people—all people—friends, neighbors, enemies, and yes, even the people we work with.

Though we can conclude that there probably were people Jesus did not like during His earthly ministry, we also know that He loved those people. He died for those scribes and Pharisees, just as much as He died for His disciples. And because He died for them, we know He loved them. So, though we are not required to like everyone we know, we are required by Scripture to love them.

But when you run into these unlikable people, you feel as though you've hit the spiritual brick wall. Since we cannot like them, we usually conclude that we cannot love them either. Our thinking is that we like people before we love them. We think of "like" as the first step of "love." With that reasoning, the command of Scripture to love everyone seems impossible.

However, I have good news for all of us. We don't have to like someone to love them. To like someone means that we admire them, enjoy them, want to be like them, and benefit greatly from their presence in our life. Webster defines *like* as to "feel an attraction, tenderness or affection for" someone. I believe "liking" someone is a feeling. You can't like someone without having good feelings about them.

God would never require of us something we could not do. As Christians, because of the power that is available to us through the Holy Spirit, it is possible to love someone whom you do not like.

Defining Love

First, let's clarify the type of love we're talking about. There are three Greek words that are all translated "love":

1. *Eros* - which is love between sexes.
2. *Philos* - which is love between friends and family.
3. *Agape* - which is the kind that characterizes God. This is the love that loves because its own inherent nature is to love. That's why the Bible says, "God is love." Love is His nature.

The kind of love that we need in order to love people we don't like is agape love. This is the type of love I am referring to when I say you can love people you don't like. And, actually, if the other two types of love—eros and philos—do not at some point mature into agape love, they will eventually fall apart. Agape love is the kind that lasts over the long haul. It's the quality of love that makes marriages really work and friendships last forever. So, keep in mind, we're talking about agape love.

Agape love is not a feeling. Though we may experience nice, warm feelings as a result of agape love, it is in no way dependent on how we feel. It does not depend on how others feel about us. We can love with agape love whether the feelings are present or absent, whether they are good or bad.

Agape love is an *action*. When this type of love is described in Scripture it is always described as an action, not a feeling. The Bible tells us that we know that God loves us because He sent His Son into the world to redeem us (John 3:16). We know that Jesus loves us because He gave His life for us. The Bible says, "Greater love hath no man than this, that a man lay down his life for his friends" (John 15:13 KJV). And God says that He will know that we love Him *if* we keep His commandments (John 14:15).

God's kind of love is an action, not a feeling. Now, that really is good news, because it tells me that I can love people toward whom I do not necessarily have good feelings. I can love people toward whom I have no feelings at all. Since love is an action, not a feeling, I can obey God's command to love everyone.

Love Actions

Well, if love is an action, what actions then are love actions? First Corinthians 13 is a good place to look for a practical description of love actions. A few of these are:

Patience   When you act with patience toward someone, you are loving that person. Keep in mind that love is not a feeling, so we don't have to *feel* patient. If you act patiently, whether you feel patient or not, you are showing agape.

Kindness   Kind words are love actions. You can say something kind, even if you might feel like being sarcastic or cutting. You can act in kindness toward other people, regardless of whether you like them or not.

Lack of Jealousy   When you refuse to behave jealously or possessively, you are showing love.

Courtesy   Just plain courtesy is a love action. How often we forget good manners, like not interrupting others when they're talking, and holding the door for those behind us.

Unselfishness   Agape love acts in an unselfish manner, without pursuing selfish advantage or trampling over others in trying to get where you want.

Endurance   When others have given up and left, agape love will still be there, hanging in with someone, perhaps listening to a seemingly endless stream of complaints.

These are just a few of the many love actions available to us. Others are gentleness, compassion, tolerance—all from our Christian "wardrobe."

Perhaps you are thinking, "If I act with love toward someone when I don't feel like doing it, isn't that hypocritical?" No, I don't think so, because God's love to us is not based on our "lovableness." Remember, Jesus loved those very same scribes and Pharisees whom He so strongly denounced. He may be, and I'm sure often is, very displeased with us as individuals, yet His love is constant. Therefore, He does not require of us to have good feelings toward everyone, but rather to act in love toward everyone.

Write it on a piece of paper and tape it to your mirror, your desk, over your sink, wherever you will see it often: *Love is not a feeling; love is an action!*

Developing Love Actions

How do we get these love actions going in our lives? It's one thing to know we should love people we don't like. It's another thing to make it happen.

Paul said in his letter to the Romans that the Holy Spirit, who was given to us, has poured out the love of God within our hearts (Romans 5:5). That's where it starts, when we accept God's love and the Holy Spirit starts spreading it all through our inner selves.

Think about God's love for you. John wrote: "To us, the greatest demonstration of God's love for us has been His sending His only Son into the world to give us life through Him. We see real love, not in the fact that we loved God, but that He loved us and sent His Son to make personal atonement for our sins" (1 John 4:9,10 YOUNG CHURCHES).

And remember, God loves those people you don't like just as much as He loves you. Let God's love pour all over you and fill you. Remember how He loves you, even when you're not very lovable. That's the beginning of learning how to love other people.

A prerequisite to developing love actions toward these unlikable people in your life is to change your thinking. There's no way you can keep on thinking of how irritating they are or how thoughtless they are, or how annoying they are, and then turn around and have love actions toward them. What you think will come out in your actions.

So, remember God's love for you, change your thinking about these unlikable people in your life, and then pray for them. Sincerely, regularly pray for their welfare. As much as you know about them, pray in detail for them. Ask God to show you what love actions to take toward them. And pray for them . . . a lot! Jesus taught us to pray for our enemies, and those who despitefully use us.

As you think about each of these people you don't like, decide which love actions are appropriate for each one. Does one require a lot of patience? Does one require compassion or endurance? Then set your will to act with those love actions toward those people.

The Amazing Results

I want to tell you what happens when you start acting with love toward people you don't like.

First of all, you lose guilt—the guilt you experience when you don't like certain people. There will always be people in your life that you will not be able to "feel" love for, no matter how hard you may try. But when you realize that love is not a feeling, but an action, you know that you can still obey God and love those people by acting out love toward them, regardless of your feelings.

Second, your love actions will have an effect in most cases. That's not the reason for your love, but most often it is a result. Your actions may well bring about a change in the person to whom they are directed.

Third, you're going to get to know God's love for you in a completely new way. When you start to show agape love toward others, then God's agape love for you will become so much more real and precious.

Learning to love people you don't really like is the key to getting along with your co-workers. Instead of trying to change them, which almost never happens, change yourself instead. Instead of concentrating on how difficult they are, concentrate on how you can find ways to love them, even though you don't like them.

Of course, it's never fully perfected, never once and for all. It is an everyday commitment. But you don't want to miss this wonderful experience of loving people you don't like. Are you willing to try? Even with those people you work with who drive you crazy? You could make a covenant with God today that you are going to begin the process, and discover what it really means to show God's love to others.

Chapter Seven

The Impossible Boss

"**H**e's absolutely impossible. He has no integrity, lies continually, is deceitful and cruel."

"She's absolutely impossible. She treats people like dirt, always making others look bad in front of other people."

"He's absolutely impossible. He never listens to anyone else, thinks he knows everything, and behaves like a dictator."

"She's absolutely impossible. She doesn't know what she's doing, and won't admit it."

"He's absolutely impossible. He can't make a decision, never gets anything done, and blames all the problems on me."

"Impossible! My boss is impossible!"

How many times have you heard something like that? How many times have you said it yourself? If you haven't run into the impossible boss yet in your career, it's highly likely that you will at some time or another. Few of us escape the experience of learning to cope with a difficult boss.

What is particularly difficult about having such managers is that we cannot avoid them, and it behooves *us* to get along with *them*. When our peers or co-workers are difficult, there is usually some way of escaping them or avoiding them or telling them to "cool it." But when it comes to our managers, we are usually stuck. The only way out is to quit, or find a new position in the company, or hang in there until they move on.

Someone gave me some good advice early in my career: "It's your job to get along with the boss, not his or her job to get along with you." That may sound unfair, but it is very realistic, and it is very good advice for anyone pursuing a career. From personal experience, however, I can tell you that it can be very difficult. I, for one, did not always succeed throughout my career at getting along with my managers.

The Desire to Run Away

I keep a journal—what I call a spiritual journal—which is simply a blank book where I write what God is teaching me through His Word. I would encourage you to start this practice, if you haven't already. It has proven to be a great blessing in my life to go back and read where I've been and how God has led me. Also, it captures the lessons God teaches me—things I might otherwise forget.

It is from that journal that I can recall so clearly a time in my career when I thought I just could not work any longer for my boss. The words written in my journal were, "I can't take any more." I'm sure there are many of you who've been at that exact spot with your boss—or maybe you are now. You know what I'm talking about.

My tolerance and patience were gone. I had endured what seemed to be inordinate amounts of unreasonable and unkind treatment. Frustration reigned supreme in my life. My manager's style was to manage through intimidation and humiliation, and I was not at all competent or experienced in handling it.

As a result of the frustration, I frequently handled confrontations poorly, making matters worse. At one point I wrote in my journal, "Lord, I know that I didn't handle that encounter with my boss very well yesterday." Like the Psalmist I wanted to say, "O, that I had wings like a dove! I would fly away and be at rest. Behold, I would wander far away . . ." (Psalms 55:6, 7).

Yes, I wanted to walk out and never go back to that office. Maybe that's where you are today. Let me encourage you to read Psalm 55. The Psalmist experienced those same feelings. Don't you appreciate the openness of David in expressing his feelings? He struggles through all kinds of emotions in the psalms, and his struggles are a great help and encouragement to me. Somehow it always helps to know someone else has had the same problem you have.

And here in Psalm 55 he is experiencing the same kind of frustration that you are experiencing if you really want to run away—from your job or anything else. David expresses all these desires he has to run away and to see his enemy defeated.

Learning to Call on God

David, however, does not remain in that depressed, desperate state. In verse 16 of that same psalm, he comes to an important decision: "As for me, I shall call upon God, and the Lord will save me." And again in verse 18: "He will redeem my soul in peace from the battle which is against me."

David begins to think about something besides his own predicament. He gets his eyes and his thoughts on his God, and determines that he will call upon God to save him. He further states his conviction that God will deliver him in *peace*. As a result of this experience, David gives us some of his most beautiful words of advice and comfort: "Cast your burden upon the Lord, and He will sustain you. He will never allow the righteous to be shaken" (Psalms 55:22).

And he ends the psalm by simply saying, "But I will trust in Thee."

This is the first step in dealing with an impossible boss: Call upon the Lord. We must focus our eyes on our God, not on our boss. This takes a set of our will, and it takes much time in prayer and in God's Word. It is very important that we openly pray about our impossible boss, and ask God to give us His view of this whole situation. Read Psalm 55 and meditate on it carefully. Make sure you are willing to look at this whole situation through God's eyes. And cast your burden on the Lord; He'll keep you going. He'll keep you from quitting or running away. He will *never* allow His righteous child to be shaken.

Checking for Self-Pity

The second thing God pointed out to me was that my whole attitude was self-centered and self-pitying: "I can't take this." "This isn't fair to *me*." "I don't have to endure this kind of treatment."

I realized I had to start thinking differently. God said to me, "Mary, it really doesn't matter what inconvenience or uncomfortableness or frustration this situation causes *you*! That is not what is at issue here." My reply was, "Sure seems that way to me, Lord!" I didn't have very much perspective.

Don't be surprised to find you lack perspective when you're in the midst of this kind of situation. God knows we lack perspective, and we can so easily get caught up in the "me" part of it all. We need to allow Him to change our perspective, if that is needed.

When we can see that there is an eternal purpose in what we're going through, things look very different to us. God clearly showed me the need to change my thinking from "Poor me. What can be done to deliver me from this terrible spot?" to "How can God be glorified in this situation? What are His purposes for putting me in this place?" When I finally could look at it that way, much of the frustration left immediately.

Eternal viewpoints are wonderful, because they deliver us from the bondage of the here and now. The trouble often is that we are so caught up in our self-pity that we really don't want to give it up. Even though relinquishing that self-pity is our doorway to freedom from frustration, we've become so accustomed to being wrapped up in it, that it is almost strangely comforting (in a very warped sense). I've noticed that tendency in myself and in others. Self-pity can hold a strange attraction for us.

Maybe you need an eternal viewpoint in your situation. Perhaps you've just become consumed, as I was, with what it was doing to *you*, and you need instead to ask God about

His purpose. And you ask, not in a demanding way, but in submission. "Lord, I submit to Your will. What would You have me to learn and how can You be glorified?" That's an important step to take in dealing with an impossible boss.

Tolerance

Then God showed me some other passages in Scripture that shed more light on dealing with a difficult boss. Proverbs 25:15 says: "By forbearance a ruler may be persuaded, And a soft tongue breaks the bone." Forbearance means tolerance—or length of anger. Even if your anger is justified in your particular situation, you need to lengthen it. Stretch it out; don't have a short fuse. And, most importantly, keep a soft tongue. With forbearance and a soft tongue a ruler can be persuaded. If you want to change your boss's behavior toward you, try God's principles. They are very clearly set forth here. Be tolerant and speak with gentleness and kindness. And watch what happens.

Discernment and Persuasiveness

Another very helpful verse is Proverbs 16:21: "The wise in heart will be called discerning, And sweetness of speech increases persuasiveness." Two traits that are very helpful in dealing with an impossible boss are discernment and persuasiveness. Discernment gives us the ability to know when to say what, to see subtleties we might have missed before, to distinguish between good and bad ideas. And we certainly could use a little persuasiveness in these situations, to be convincing and influential with that difficult manager.

This Scripture tells us that the wise in heart are discerning. What does it mean to be wise in heart? We are told in 1 Corinthians 1:24 that Christ is the wisdom of God. In order to be truly wise in heart, we must have Christ and the Spirit of Christ dwelling within us. Without Him there is no real wisdom. So, we need to constantly be learning more of Jesus, and that comes from the Word of God. We have to be saturated with Jesus in order to be wise in heart.

And in James 3:17 we read that "the wisdom from above is first pure, then peaceable, gentle, reasonable, full of mercy and good fruits, unwavering, without hypocrisy." Test your ideas and your attitudes toward your boss by these criteria: pure, peaceable, gentle, reasonable, full of mercy and goodness, unwavering, without hypocrisy. That's the kind of wisdom that will make us discerning.

Then, once again, we must check our speech out if we want to be persuasive. Tough talk, belligerent words, hostile confrontations and contentiousness will not increase our persuasiveness. But words that are easy to swallow—palatable, sweet words—these will make us much more persuasive in dealing with our management. We need to think of ways to make our ideas acceptable; think of ways to make our speech pleasing and good tasting.

Putting Aside Malice

Malice is the desire to see something bad happen to someone. Oh, how easy it is to fall into that trap when you are working for a difficult manager. Since we cannot usually express our displeasure to them, we can let our imagination run wild with thoughts of all kinds of misfortune: We wish they would make a big mistake and get caught. We wish they would get fired. We wish higher management would see how bad they are.

There are several Scriptures that warn us about malice:

> *But now you also, put them all aside: anger, wrath, malice, slander, and abusive speech from your mouth.*
>
> Colossians 3:8

> *Therefore, putting aside all malice and all guile and hypocrisy and envy and all slander.*
>
> 1 Peter 2:1

> *Let all bitterness and wrath and anger and clamor and slander be put away from you, along with all malice.*
>
> Ephesians 4:31

It is pretty clear from these passages that malice has to be dealt with decisively. It is easy to have those malicious thoughts without realizing how sinful and harmful they are. Paul and Peter give us strong admonitions to get rid of malice—put it aside, take it off. Again, by an act of our will, not our emotions. We have to take off that malice toward our difficult boss. Whether they ever change or not, we must obey God. And it is clear that there is no place in a Christian's life for malice.

Learning to Endure Wrong Treatment

The Bible has much to say about how employees should treat their managers and how managers should treat their employees, and the following is a classic passage:

Servants, be submissive to your masters with all respect, not
only to those who are good and gentle, but also to those who
are unreasonable. For this finds favor, if for the sake of con-
science toward God a man bears up under sorrows when
suffering unjustly. For what credit is there if, when you sin
and are harshly treated, you endure it with patience? But if
when you do what is right and suffer for it you patiently en-
dure it, this finds favor with God. For you have been called
for this purpose, since Christ also suffered for you, leaving
you an example for you to follow in His steps, who commit-
ted no sin, nor was any deceit found in His mouth; and
while being reviled He did not revile in return; while suf-
fering, He uttered no threats, but kept entrusting Himself to
Him who judges righteously; and He Himself bore our sins
in His body on the cross, that we might die to sin and live to
righteousness; for by His wounds you were healed.

                                                   1 Peter 2:18–25

Yielding to Authority

It is really important that all of us employees understand
and obey this principle given to us by Peter. First, he tells us
we are to submit to our masters with all respect, and not just
to the nice ones but also to those who are unreasonable.

How do we do that? Submit means to yield to the authority of another; to be obedient. That's the first step—
yield to the authority of your boss, with *respect*. I can hear
some of you asking, "How can you act with respect toward
someone whom you really do not respect?" The same way
you can love someone you don't like, as we discussed in
chapter 6.

Respect means, in addition to other things, to treat with consideration. And you *can* do that even if your feelings are contrary. Remember, we cannot run by our emotions. That will get us into trouble every time. We must set our will to do what is right, and let the emotions go. You must *will* to respect that unreasonable boss and to be obedient to him or her.

Maintaining Excellent Performance

The second thing that I learn from this passage is that I must make sure I am doing my duty, and that I am not in any way to blame for the unpleasantness my manager is demonstrating. You see, what Peter goes on to say in this passage is that it is commendable if we bear up under unfair treatment. That kind of suffering finds favor with God. Now I ask you, wouldn't you like to know that God is pleased with you and finds favor with you? That is truly special recognition. Well, it can be yours if you endure this difficult situation with your boss by doing your duty and being patient.

However, if part of the problem is that you're not doing your work well, or you're not being obedient, or you're not motivated as highly as you should be, then what credit is it, Peter says, if you endure the harsh treatment you are receiving? You're simply enduring what you deserve, and that gets no special recognition.

But if, indeed, you are doing your duty, and you still must bear patiently with a difficult and impossible boss, you are doing something very worthwhile in God's sight.

Sharing the Sufferings of Christ

Why is this kind of suffering so precious to God? Peter goes on to tell us it is because that is the way Christ suffered, and when we endure unjust treatment with patience and tolerance, we are sharing in His suffering. That is the example that Christ left us. He did not talk back when He was falsely accused. He didn't offer tit for tat. He didn't threaten anyone, but He kept entrusting Himself to God.

Can you trust your impossible work situation to God? Can you keep on trusting it to His care, even though it seems entirely wrong to you?

Peter says we are called to suffer unjustly! Can you believe that? When this passage was first becoming real to me, I said, "Lord, that is really tough—*called* to suffer unjustly! I don't want to be treated unfairly."

Don't feel guilty if you have that reaction. None of us in the flesh can *want* to suffer unjustly. None of us would ask for it or seek after it. But though I didn't want to be treated unfairly, I did want to follow in the steps of Christ and find favor with God. Therefore, I could truthfully say, "Lord, I want to follow You and obey You and please You. Therefore, if it is to Your glory for me to continue enduring this impossible boss, I accept it not because I look forward to it, but because I want to please You."

The Results of Peter's Principle

Let me tell you what starts to happen when you change your thinking and your attitude and apply Peter's principle to your working world. The sting goes out of the situation.

Your boss may continue to be impossible, but with an eternal viewpoint and a different motivation, it won't get to you the way it used to. I'm not saying it will be pleasant, but it just will not upset you anymore.

I can testify to this. I couldn't believe the changes I saw in myself. As I continued to apply these principles to my situation, I was amazed to realize that this particular, impossible boss just could not get to me anymore. I didn't take things personally, I didn't get upset, I didn't think of it once I walked out of the office. The sting was gone; and when the sting goes, it isn't that difficult to endure.

Does the Bible have any practical help when we're faced with an impossible boss? Oh, yes indeed. However, it probably isn't what you'd like to hear. Our human natures would rather have sympathy and pity and condolence and retribution and revenge.

But the miracle is that God's principles work and our way doesn't. We are called to die to our natural selves, and death never seems attractive. But when we do, then we can be alive to God. That death to self that you dread so much is really your avenue to freedom and peace.

My friend Joan experienced an unfair situation recently at her job. Someone else was given a promotion that truly should have been her's. And she was upset; who wouldn't be? She wanted to go in and tell her boss off and tell the other girl off and let them know that she knew she had been had. She was angry.

I said to her, "Can you go back in there and love that girl, and treat her especially well? Can you keep your mouth closed and not defend yourself or seek revenge? Can you maintain respect for your boss's authority, even though he has treated you wrongly?"

I pointed out to her that if she behaved that way she would have an undeniable witness in that office. After all, everyone else knew that she had gotten a bad deal, and they all knew how they would react if it happened to them. So they were looking for the same kind of reaction from her.

But if, instead, they saw her react with kindness and love and a gentle spirit, they would have to take notice. How could that be explained? How could she do that?

Joan went back and did the right thing. She was kind to the girl who got the promotion, and she didn't let her boss have it. The next time I saw her, I asked how it went. She reported that she had applied this biblical principle, and somehow the promotion didn't really seem so important to her anymore.

A couple of weeks later she reported that she was actually thankful she didn't get that promotion, because it required lots of overtime and the girl in the job was having quite a bit of trouble. Joan could see that God had protected her from a very difficult position.

I asked her, "Who won? You died to yourself and you did what was totally contrary to your human desires. But tell me, who won?" She looked at me, and quietly said, "I did."

Why are we so slow to learn that principle? We are the winners when we go God's way—even to the point of dying to ourselves. He is not a cruel taskmaster. He has told us that His yoke is easy and His burden is light. Our method will not be easy. If we insist on doing things our way and carrying the load all by ourselves, it will not be a light load. It will be heavy and dreary and terribly difficult.

Accepting an Impossible Boss

Can you thank God for putting that impossible boss in your life in order to lead you into a deeper life of trust in Him? With eternity's values in mind, can you agree that it is more important to learn more about God and His love for you, and to grow in grace and faith in Him, than it is to be delivered from an impossible boss?

It is not easy to accept that impossible boss. In no way would I represent that this kind of unjust suffering is a piece of cake. But I do believe that accepting it from God's hands, and letting Him guide us in our reactions—even to the point of suffering unjustly—is easier than our normal human reactions of anger and bitterness and vengeance.

Chapter Eight

Dealing
With Men
on the Job

When my daughter was entering her sophomore year in high school, she chose an all-girl school to attend. For those last three years, her school and social environment was almost exclusively female. When she chose her college, however, she made sure it was coeducational. Can you blame her? Three years in an environment without boys was enough!

Let's face it, for the most part we like to have men around. Life could be pretty dull if we never interacted with the opposite sex. I'm sure, for the most part, men share that view with us.

This attraction we feel toward men is very normal. It is a part of our makeup and part of God's plan to have two sexes, attracted to each other, different in many ways and yet quite complementary to each other.

As we begin to interact with the opposite sex, we instinctively recognize that there are differences. We begin to learn from an early age how to get along with the male species, as we encounter brothers, fathers, boy friends, dates, sweethearts, husbands. We experience these male/female relationships in many different environments, including home, school, church, social situations.

Then we enter the working world, and we face the challenge of interacting with men in this setting. With women moving into the work force at an accelerated rate, holding positions previously available only to men, that interaction has become more evident and more frequent. Women are finding themselves in very male environments, surrounded by men, daily engaged with men as peers, as managers, as subordinates.

And frequently we are not aware of the dynamics of these male/female relationships; many of us are in unfamiliar territory. I remember when I began my career as a sales representative for IBM. I was the only female in my office, and I can still see that large sales office, jammed with desks to accommodate about forty sales people, and there I was in the middle, surrounded by men on every side. Sounds like a dream come true for a single woman, you say? Well, while I certainly enjoyed the attention that my unique situation afforded me, I discovered quite quickly that I was not prepared to deal with the many diverse complications that arose from the male/female aspect of it.

Having made a great many mistakes in this area of my business life, I know how easy it is to make the wrong moves and deal with these male/female encounters inappropriately. Therefore, I think it is important to address this subject very directly and candidly, because many of you are still struggling with this very problem.

Male Friendships on the Job

What about those nice, well-balanced men that we enjoy working with and for? It *is* possible to develop friendships with men you work with. I can think of several men I've worked with whom I consider good friends. As it happens, they're all married. I'm also very good friends with their wives and families. All social contact is with the men and their wives, since they are married. We should be very careful never to give the wives of men with whom we work any reason to distrust our relationships with their husbands. It is our responsibility to exercise extreme caution in order to eliminate the possibility of causing them any unnecessary concern.

Male Subordinates

With more and more women now holding management positions, it is no longer uncommon to find women managers with men reporting to them. This has broken new ground for men and women, and frequently presents problems for these women managers in knowing just how to relate to their subordinates.

I've encountered many women who are struggling with a very basic question in this regard, and that question is: Should a Christian woman hold a position of leadership over men? The question is an outgrowth of the strong conviction of many evangelical Christians that women should not have leadership roles over men within the church. This position is based on passages in 1 Corinthians 14:34, 35 and 1 Timothy 2:9–15.

Christian women who have been immersed in this conviction that it is wrong to hold leadership positions over men in the church environment quite naturally question whether that principle extends to all leadership positions, including the business world. It is a legitimate question, and it should be confronted.

At this point, I will not get into the question of leadership roles for women in the church, but will limit myself to working environments. As I look at Scripture, I can find no directive to women that would prohibit them from holding management positions, including positions of leadership over men.

To the contrary, I can think of many women within Scripture who did hold leadership positions. Deborah was a judge over her nation, and she led an army of men into battle (Judges 3 and 4). The Proverbs Woman (Proverbs 31) had both a manufacturing and a real estate business, which easily could have put her in a position of directing male subordinates. We know she managed her household of many servants, and presumably that would include male servants. Lydia was a seller of purple (Acts 16), which was a most prestigious position. She must have interacted with men and directed them at times. We know she had a large household under her management, and this household would most likely have included men.

With no biblical directive to prohibit women from leadership positions on the job, I believe a Christian woman is free to hold management positions with male subordinates, if she desires to do so and has the opportunity. There is no reason to feel guilty about it or apologize for it.

However, these female management positions can be difficult at times, as we learn how to deal with the men who report to us. For most of us women, this new role of managing men is so new that we can easily make some basic mistakes in these relationships. Let me point out a few areas here that could present problems.

Because the territory is so new, many of us overreact by trying to be too assertive and working too hard at establishing our authority. We are naturally a little insecure in these new roles, and it is easy to overcompensate by being too rigid and demanding.

On the other hand, some women bend over too far backward to keep from intimidating male subordinates and to avoid coming on too strong, and this can cause us to be weak managers who lack proper control.

We need to find that natural, happy medium that allows us to be ourselves, to manage effectively in our own style, without being overly aware of the fact that we are female and they are male. As much as possible, we need to learn to manage from a manager's point of view, not a female point of view.

In my prayer manual I have a list of areas in my life to which I know I am easily vulnerable, things that I recognize as possible satanic strongholds in my life. One is a tendency to overreact, and I continually ask God to deliver me from that propensity. I think as female managers dealing with male subordinates we easily can overreact either by being too tough as we struggle to establish our authority, or too lenient as we fear being tagged a "pushy broad."

Make it a matter of prayer that God will show you how to walk that middle line, that you may find your own balance as a manager, and that you may not overreact in dealing with male subordinates.

When we encounter male subordinates who resent having a female manager, we have a delicate situation on our hands. This is certainly an appropriate time to ask for special wisdom from God, as He has promised us in James 1:5. Patience and endurance will likely be required of us.

There is no reason to be intimidated by these male subordinates, and we have a responsibility to require adequate performance from them. After all, if you are their manager, you have earned your position and they must learn to respect that. But your best hope of winning their respect and dispelling their negative attitude toward you in most cases is to ignore their attitude as much as possible, and manage them as you would any other employee. If you are fair and kind in your dealings with them, as a Christian should always be, while at the same time doing the best job possible in your own position, they will more often than not change their attitude toward you. It may take more time than you would like, but it can happen.

Try to put yourself in your employees' shoes, and recognize that there could be any number of reasons for their behavior. They may feel threatened by having a woman manager, or their background could have prejudiced them against women in business. Whatever their reasons, instead of getting angry at them or vindictive, ask God to give you compassion and tolerance. It is a wonderful opportunity to demonstrate the difference that Jesus Christ makes in our lives.

The men may expect you to behave in a defensive, aggressive manner, but when they see the patience and gentleness of the Holy Spirit in your behavior, they will be at a loss to explain it. It may well give you an opportunity to "give an account for the hope that is in you, yet with gentleness and reverence," as we read in 1 Peter 3:15.

A verse that God has again and again brought to my attention in these difficult situations is Proverbs 16:21: "Sweetness of speech increases persuasiveness." It really is important for us to watch the way we talk in these sensitive situations, and to remember to make our speech palatable. Find ways to make your directions and your ideas easy to handle for these male subordinates. It won't diminish your stature to go out of your way to ease the tension for them. And it will increase your persuasiveness. It is a biblical principle I've proven in my own life time and again.

The Possibility of an Attraction

In a male/female business relationship, because of our natural tendency to be attracted to the opposite sex, and because of the amount of time spent together on a daily basis, an attraction may very well occur. Most of us have seen this happen or have experienced it ourselves. What does a Christian working woman do when she feels an attraction to a male co-worker?

The Critical Question

The very first moment you have any inkling that you may be developing an attraction for a man on your job or he for you, ask yourself one critical question: Is either of you married?

When One or Both Are Married. If the answer to that question is yes, your course of action is very simple and clear. It may not be easy, but it certainly is simple and uncomplicated. The principle set forth in the Bible is unequiv-

ocal: People who are married can allow no intimate relationships with people of the opposite sex. If either party is married, there is one clear course for you as a Christian. You
cannot allow any words or feelings or looks or innuendos to
be exchanged between you and this man. That is it! Final! If
it means changing jobs or asking to be transferred, do it.
There is no middle ground.

You may think it unnecessary to emphasize such an obvious truth, but as Christian women in a society that gives
very little respect or regard to marriage vows, we have to
remind ourselves of these basic Christian principles from
time to time. Have you noticed how easy it is for us to lower
our standards to those of the world around us, instead of
motivating others to raise their standards to those of God's
Word?

It would be nice if these attractions only happened to single, available people, but that is not the case. I have happily
married friends in the working world, who still must be on
their guard against an attraction developing with men in
their work environment.

Let me hasten to add that these attractions are certainly
not limited to working women. They are possible whether
or not a woman leaves her home every morning to go to
work. However, it is fair to say that most working women
meet and interact with more men than women who do not
work, and therefore the opportunities for developing these
attractions are more prevalent. That simply means, that as
Christian working women, we must be very aware of the
dangers that could await us.

The answer is the same even if one of the people involved
is experiencing a difficult marriage. Many times couples

tend to justify illegitimate relationships by rationalizing that one of them is in a very unhappy marriage. The condition of the marriage in no way changes the principle by which Christians should abide. As Christians we should do everything possible to help hurting marriages find healing. Allowing a relationship to develop with a person whose marriage is shaky will do just the opposite.

In today's society such a position appears to be very drastic, legalistic, eccentric, and inflexible. But that's because we have become so infiltrated with the world's philosophy, that basic Christian principles now appear unrealistic. Remember, God's principles work. While they are ageless, they are not outdated; they are not old-fashioned. That is simply Satan's lie, which many people have bought.

Interestingly enough, you will note that male/female relationships today seem to have rougher going than ever. Society has accepted and adopted new rules for these relationships, where living together is totally acceptable, instant intimacy without any commitment is expected, loyalty to marriage vows is considered unworkable, and total sexual freedom is the order of the day. This appeals to our human flesh; it sounds like a life-style that will offer freedom and happiness; it is made to appear sophisticated and normal. However, with all this liberal thinking, there is more unhappiness and discontent with relationships than ever.

You would think we would see that fact, and admit that this new sexual freedom has only increased our problems. But instead, people grope for new freedoms, new experiences, new answers, never willing to face the fact that those time-honored standards of conduct for relationships are the only ones that give stability and true freedom.

Satan is a master liar, and he wants us to think that we cannot be happy or contented living under God's principles. But he cannot make good on his promises. All of us could tell of many people we know or perhaps our own experience where many lives have been harmed and ruined by disobeying this Christian principle. Satan makes people believe that he can give them more happiness and fulfillment if they will do it his way, but he never delivers on his promises.

So, if you are attracted to a man with whom you work, or he is attracted to you, and either of you is married, you don't even need to pray about what you should do. When God's Word gives a clear answer, there is no need to ask for *special* guidance. He will *never* lead us individually in a direction that is contrary to His written Word.

The only acceptable course of action for a Christian is to discontinue the relationship and avoid any further possibility of allowing that attraction to increase. And the break must be drastic and definite. If you think you can have long talks, quiet lunches, or innocent encounters in such a relationship without ever allowing it out of bounds, you don't understand chemistry too well or you have too much confidence in yourself. It isn't only a question of that chemistry getting out of hand. A nonsexual relationship that becomes emotionally intimate to the point that it takes something away from the marriage is a form of unfaithfulness.

Don't be fooled by rationalizing that you are just being a good friend. You will be opening yourself to immense temptation and chances are you will succumb. Many times illegitimate relationships begin because one of those involved is a good listener. How many times have I heard a woman say, "He didn't have anyone else he could talk with. I was the only friend he had, and I just couldn't be cold and unkind to him."

If he needs help and counseling, you are the wrong person to give it. Certainly it is possible for him to find help in other places and people. That excuse just will not hold water. There is no good reason for you to ever allow a wrong relationship to develop.

Many times we women are allured by male attention, particularly if there is no other male in our life at the time. And we begin to enjoy the nice feeling of having a male presence in our life and want to forget that it is an improper relationship. That is a very easy trap for us to fall into.

No matter how flattering it may be to you to have that male attention, forget it. Drop it, and drop it fast. The sooner you do it, the better. Take whatever drastic steps are necessary to insure that you are not tempted to let that relationship develop beyond the professional and business level. To do anything else is to give Satan a foothold in your life. Remember, Satan never delivers on his promises. He will make that male attention look very attractive, but in the end it will turn into much trouble and heartache for you.

Ephesians 4:27 warns us that we should not give the devil any opportunity to get a foothold in our lives. Proverbs 4:26, 27 says, "Watch the path of your feet, And all your ways will be established. Do not turn to the right nor to the left; Turn your foot from evil." The correct course of action is very clear for a Christian. It is our responsibility to keep our feet riveted to the right path, not turning for an instant to the right or to the left.

Jesus said:

> *If your hand or your foot causes you to stumble, cut it off and throw it from you; it is better for you to enter life crippled or lame, than having two hands or two feet, to be cast into the eternal fire. And if your eye causes you to stumble, pluck it out, and throw it from you. It is better for you to enter life with one eye, than having two eyes, to be cast into the hell of fire.*
>
> Matthew 18:8,9

When Both Are Single   But suppose you are single and so is he. Then what do you do when you're attracted to a man with whom you work? Assuming that he is a Christian, because you would not ever want to be seriously interested in a man who was not, you need to think through very carefully the effect of having a relationship with a co-worker.

There is no scriptural guideline on this one, but common sense tells us that such a relationship can cause complications. It tends to distract you from your job, and other co-workers may resent it if they feel it is affecting your work or their work load. It is almost impossible to keep these relationships quiet; usually everyone is aware. You may think no one knows, but that is rarely the case.

Certainly, if one of you is in management and the other is not, you will be exposing yourself to widespread criticism. That kind of situation can easily lead to conflict of interest, or conversely, you may bend over so far backward to avoid conflict of interest, that your own career could suffer as a result.

If it appears that this relationship may become established and regular, it might be a good idea for one of you to try to change jobs or departments. You'll be able to work in a more relaxed fashion, do a better job, and enjoy your relationship with more freedom.

I do know of an instance, however, where two single people were able to keep a relationship totally separate from their work environment, and they worked together as peers for two or three years without a problem. They were both very mature people, who never talked about the relationship at work, rarely had lunch together or socialized on the job whatsoever. When their careers eventually led them to different departments, though, it was much more comfortable for both of them.

Try to be objective if you find yourself in such circumstances. Find someone who knows the situation and can be trusted, and ask for counsel. This is a case where other respected opinions would be very useful to you.

In summary, if we approach this male/female part of our business lives with a commitment to uphold the name of Jesus Christ, and to make certain that nothing in our lives brings dishonor to Him, we will have the appropriate attitude, and He will give us guidance as we work our way through what can often be "touchy" situations. We are living in enemy territory, so to speak, for we are not of this world, though we are in it, as Jesus has told us in John 17:15,16. Therefore, in a sense we are in a fishbowl in our working worlds, on view for all to see if our claim of Christianity makes any real difference in our lives.

It is a wonderful opportunity to show a watching world that Christ is a reality. But we must live extremely circumspect lives, avoiding any appearance of evil. A passage from

1 Peter 2:12 and 15 gives us a very clear directive in this respect:

> *Live such good lives among the pagans that, though they ac-*
> *cuse you of doing wrong, they may see your good deeds and*
> *glorify God on the day he visits us. For it is God's will that*
> *by doing good you should silence the ignorant talk of foolish*
> *men (NIV).*

The world is watching us once we declare ourselves followers of the Lord. Our lives, then, must be lived in such a manner that they cannot, though they try, accuse us truthfully of wrongful lives.

I believe that particularly in this area of relating to men on the job we must be especially certain that our behavior is circumspect. Go the extra mile, where necessary. Leave no room for doubt. Remember, you carry the reputation of Jesus Christ with you; you are His representative. It is a marvelous, and at the same time grave, responsibility. We must not take it lightly.

Chapter Nine

Profanity, Off-Color Jokes, and Sexual Propositions

Some of us try to act as though we didn't hear it; some of us "grin" our way through, hoping no one will notice how uncomfortable we are; some of us blast out in loud protest, embarrassing and alienating people in the process. Profanity and suggestive conversation are difficult to avoid in the working world, and often we just don't know how to deal with them.

As I think back over my work experience, I realize that I've reacted in all of those ways at one time or another. When I was just starting in my sales career, I tried very hard to be accepted by everyone, so I never objected to any language used in my presence for fear of alienating someone. In fact, sadly, I was a participant at times during those years when I was running from God. At other times I've shifted in my chair uncomfortably, not knowing how to react to a dirty joke (and sometimes I still do!). Occasionally I've ob-

157

jected in a manner that labeled me "Miss Goodie-Two-Shoes," which was not an effective way to deal with the problem, either.

The Acceptance of Profanity

There aren't too many of us who can escape a working environment where profanity and other inappropriate conversation are present. Our society has made it very acceptable for almost any language to be used in almost any setting. Over the years I've noticed that more and more people are using profanity, particularly women. It's very commonplace, and it's not limited to less-educated people. In fact, I think profanity has assumed a level of acceptance whereby using it identifies one as somewhat sophisticated and sociable.

It's almost laughable when you think about it, because the use of profanity really indicates a lack of individuality, a lack of self-control, a lack of good taste, and a limited vocabulary—traits that are not attractive in successful business people. Yet when it comes to the language that is used, these common, low, demeaning, vulgar, trite words and expressions have come to be acceptable and even expected in most working environments.

And because profanity is so acceptable and commonplace, I think many Christians are intimidated by it, or have become so accustomed to it that they rarely express any opposition. In fact, sad to say, I fear many Christians hear it so much that they lose sight of its evil and eventually participate themselves.

Is the Bible Really Relevant?

Well, what are we supposed to do? This is a modern-day problem, and there's nothing in the Bible that tells us how to handle these contemporary situations. Right? Isn't that the way we think sometimes—that the Bible is out of place and outdated when it comes to business or work environments? Certainly the world around us thinks that way, and quite frequently we Christians fall right in step.

A non-Christian friend of mine once told me that I was foolish to think that I could apply a Bible principle to a specific situation I was facing on my job. "You're carrying this stuff too far, Mary," he told me. "It won't work in the business world."

And you know, for a minute he intimidated me, and I did feel rather foolish and naive. Then God gently reminded me of 1 Corinthians 2:14, which says that a natural person does not accept the things of the Spirit of God; for they are foolishness to him, and he cannot understand them because they are spiritually appraised.

So, we shouldn't be surprised to find the attitude prevalent among our peers and co-workers that the Bible is irrelevant to our current business environment. But those of us who have accepted Jesus Christ as our personal Savior have the Spirit of God within us, who gives us the power to appraise spiritually any situation we face, and we'll find that God's Word is not outdated or out of place in dealing with work situations.

Biblical Principles

Well, what are some principles or guidelines to help us in dealing with the people around us who continually use profanity and tell off-color jokes; whose general conversation is suggestive and inappropriate? And how do we as women deal with sexual propositions or suggestions?

The first thing is to make absolutely certain that we are in no way participants. Without any doubt, this kind of talk is totally off limits for a Christian who desires to be truly committed to Jesus Christ. Two of the many passages that deal with our language are appropriate here:

> In all things show yourself to be an example of good deeds, with purity in doctrine, dignified, sound in speech which is beyond reproach, in order that the opponent may be put to shame, having nothing bad to say about us.
>
> Titus 2:7,8

> Let no one look down on your youthfulness, but rather in speech, conduct, love, faith and purity, show yourself an example of those who believe.
>
> 1 Timothy 4:12

Our speech should be a distinguishing mark of our Christianity. In an environment where profanity is common and accepted, we, as Christians, should stand out as light does in darkness. It should be quickly obvious that we *never* engage in any kind of talk or conversation or joke that even comes close to being off-color or impure. No one we work with should ever be able to remember hearing a profane word come out of our mouths.

This is a cut and dried, black and white area, clearly set

forth in Scripture, and we must obey without any thought as to the consequences. We shouldn't even stop to worry about how we will be perceived if our language is different from everyone else's because we never use profane or inappropriate language. Regardless of whether they think of us as religious fanatics, or whatever reaction it may cause, our course is still clear: In no way should any questionable language proceed from our mouths.

That is the first guideline in dealing with profanity. In many cases, as your peers become aware that you never participate in the slightest bit of off-color language or jokes, it will dry up when you're around. If you notice that people change the subject when you walk in, or apologize for bad language in your presence, I think it should be considered as a compliment. Your testimony should be that clear.

Appropriate Responses to Profanity

However, many times people care not at all if you're offended, and indeed may step up their level of profanity just because they know it bothers you. What are some other steps you can take to combat this kind of environment?

Stan had worked for many years for his firm. He had a lot of seniority and a good job. Suddenly the company was sold, and there was a complete change in the personnel of top management. Stan was asked to stay, but before too long he had a good offer from another company. It was a hard decision for him to make. His old job was near home; he had lots of friends at work—and there were all those years invested in the company. One day Stan came out of a meeting, very much like many under the new management, with his mind made up—to leave. The language used at the meetings was coarse beyond belief. Stan just wasn't comfortable there anymore.

If you're in a particularly offensive environment, getting out of it may be your best course of action, as it was for Stan. No job is worth subjecting yourself to continual coarse language.

Aside from changing jobs, there are other ways to deal with profanity, inappropriate conversations, and dirty jokes. First, anything you say or do must come from a heart of love and compassion, not from an attitude of "holier than thou." It cannot come in a condemning way, and should not put the offenders on the spot or make them look bad, if at all possible. Pray for these people and ask God to give you His love and compassion for them.

Here are some suggestions: When others use the name of our precious Lord as profanity, which is the worst kind of profanity, stop them quietly and gently ask if they know Him. They will usually look at you and say, "What?" And you simply say, "Well, you use His name an awful lot, and I just wondered if you really know Him—Jesus Christ? I know Him—He's my Savior, my friend, my Lord. So, since I know how wonderful He is, I have to believe that you've never really gotten to know Him, or you wouldn't be able to use His name in such a degrading manner."

Now, something along that line will either stop them cold, and cause them to change the subject, or could open up an opportunity to explain to them who Jesus really is. But it must be done gently, without a condemning attitude.

Another possibility is to say, "You know, if you used my mother's name as a curse word, I wouldn't hesitate to stop and object very strongly. But I'm sure you would have too much respect to use my mother's name in a degrading way. Yet, Jesus Christ is far more precious to me than even my mother, and it really is painful to me to hear you use His name as a curse word."

Lou, a lawyer, handles this kind of profanity by asking if people realize what the Bible says about the end result of using God's name in vain. He reminds them of the second commandment, which says that anyone who takes God's name in vain will not go unpunished. He approaches it as though doing them a favor, to alert them to the consequences of their actions, rather than that he is offended at their language. That's a strong approach, but if you knew Lou, you could well imagine how effectively he could carry it off.

Why the Name of Jesus Christ?

Frequently when I object to the use of our Lord's name, I say, "Why do you use *His* name? There are many other people in history whose names you could use. Why not George Washington, or King Henry IV, or Mohammed or Buddha? Why do you only use Jesus Christ as a curse word?"

That really makes people stop and think. They will usually reply that it's just a bad habit. But now the door is open for you to explain that the name of Jesus is a name more highly honored by God than any other name. And we know from Scripture that someday at His name every knee shall bow and every tongue confess that He is Lord (*see* Philippians 2:9,10).

It is for this reason, of course, that through the ages our enemy, Satan, has done everything possible to damage and harm the name of Jesus Christ. He knows that there is power and forgiveness and new life in that name, and he wants to destroy it. He hates the name of Jesus.

If you explain why Jesus' name is used rather than any other historical or religious person, it gives you a wonderful opportunity to talk about our Savior. It could be an effective opening for a witness.

Dealing with Vulgar Language and Jokes

Words and jokes that are just distasteful and vulgar, though offensive, do not demand the same bold stand that the use of our Lord's name does, and I rarely say anything against it. I simply avoid it as much as possible. Sometimes it may be appropriate to use body language and facial expressions to show that we consider such remarks inappropriate.

When I'm caught in a group from which I cannot escape—such as a meeting—and an off-color joke is told, I usually just endure it. But I in no way show any approval or acceptance of the joke. We are not required to appreciate these kinds of jokes or remarks, even when they come from upper management. In situations where it's possible for me to leave, I try to leave as quietly as possible, and simply remove myself from the environment.

If you're encountering peers or co-workers who insist on telling dirty jokes in your presence, and it's not possible to escape, you may find it appropriate to address them directly about it, and simply request that they wait until you're out of earshot to repeat their jokes. It is difficult to do this without coming off as "Suzy Spiritual," and we don't want to be offensive if we can avoid it.

Jesus' Instructions and Example

But I'm reminded that our Lord didn't worry about offending people in cases where He felt the issue was important enough. Many times He stated His opposition to things and people, and His words were strong and undeniably offensive. His purpose was not to offend people, but rather to defend what He knew demanded His defense.

The beautiful balance of our Lord is a role model of how we should act and react in offensive circumstances. There certainly are times that call for righteous anger and indignation, and there are other times when a quiet and gentle reaction is the best course.

It all requires prayer and sensitivity on our part. If you're in the midst of these kinds of circumstances, give it a great deal of prayer time, and be sure you remain compassionate and kind. If you are belligerent toward the people involved, you probably need to work on your attitude first.

It's very important that we don't assume the appearance of condemnation. We don't want to project the attitude that Christianity is totally negative, or that Christians are just purists and killjoys. It is a fine line to walk, and requires much prayer.

The issue is not that our Christian ears cannot tolerate this language, or that we are contaminated by it. Jesus said that though we are in this world, we are not of it. He further prayed to His Father not that we should be removed from this world, but that we should be kept from the evil one (John 17:14–16). It is not His purpose to shield us from every worldly environment. Rather, He has purposed to leave us here in the midst of this worldly environment as witnesses.

That means that we will be subjected to hearing and seeing things contrary to our beliefs and God's standards. But we can learn a wonderful trick of "tuning out" and focusing our minds on good things when surrounded by bad language. And sometimes that is more appropriate than a verbal response.

I just wonder if when the Lord was eating with the notorious sinners of His day, He heard language that was inappropriate? That wouldn't be surprising, and I would imagine that if He did, He handled it very tactfully and gently. I could imagine at some times He might not even rebuke people for those vulgar words and phrases which were a part of their everyday conversation. He knew that their hearts had to be changed first, and His presence would soon send a message that this Man was not ordinary, and ordinary language was not acceptable.

The Familiar Double Standard

Quite often I have had colleagues apologize to me for the use of bad language in my presence, whether from them or someone else. They seemed to feel that bad language was reserved for men only.

Now, in a sense I appreciate the fact that they identify me as a lady who doesn't approve of bad language. But on more than one occasion I have said, "If the language is inappropriate for my ears, it is just as inappropriate for male ears."

Women don't have particularly sensitive ears that cannot accept what men's ears can. This is a double standard which just doesn't make sense. Good taste and appropriate language are the same for male and female, so this eliminates the need for two sets of vocabularies—one when women are present and one when they're not. I find that kind of double standard very hypocritical and indefensible.

Sexual Advances

Sexual remarks and suggestions are another problem we may have to deal with on the job. Let me say categorically that the response to these situations should be the same, no matter where they're encountered, and that is an unqualified, unhesitating "NO!" If you ever stop to consider whether it might harm your career to take a firm stand, you've opened the door for trouble.

How many women have you and I known who've gotten themselves involved with men they work with because of a hesitation on their part to turn a man off for fear it would damage their career? And Christian women are not immune to these temptations.

Proverbs 4 gives us very strong admonitions about dealing with evil suggestions:

> Do not enter the path of the wicked, And do not proceed in the way of evil men. Avoid it, do not pass by it; Turn away from it and pass on (14,15).
> Let your eyes look directly ahead, And let your gaze be fixed straight in front of you. Watch the path of your feet, And all your ways will be established. Do not turn to the right nor to the left; Turn your foot from evil (25–27).

I think the writer here is trying to tell us that if we give an evil idea the smallest opportunity, we're really asking for trouble. There's one proper response to sexual suggestions or overtures for a Christian woman, and it is an unqualified, "No way!"

Don't for one minute be flattered by these suggestions or advances. That's something to which we women are very vulnerable, and "sweet talk" can turn our heads quickly. An illicit suggestion, coated in the right words, can sound rather attractive. Remember Proverbs 4, and don't give it one second's thought. If you have to make a mistake in a situation like this, make sure it's on the side of overreacting! Make certain your message is clear: The answer is no now, and it will always be no.

Can we, as Christians in the working world, take a firm, yet loving stand against vulgar and inappropriate language, profanity, off-color jokes? I trust you agree with me that the answer is definitely yes. However, without question, it requires much careful thought and sensitivity on our part.

If you find yourself faced with these problems, pray about them. Then try some of the above suggestions for dealing with them.

Remember, we are called to be salt and light in a dark and tasteless world, and the difference in our lives should be visible to all. A difference that makes others want what we have, rather than turning them off.

Chapter Ten

Pressure
and
Fatigue

Do you constantly find yourself faced with thirty hours worth of work and twenty-four hours worth of day? Is that pressure and fatigue more than you can handle at times?

I think working women are very prone to finding themselves in the predicament of being overworked, overcommitted, tired, and exhausted. A lot is expected of us. Many of us not only hold down demanding jobs, but run a household, as well. We have husbands, and children, and housework, and all that they demand. Some of us are single mothers, and do all that work without anyone at home to help share the responsibility. And those of us who are single often have responsibility for aging parents, as well as our home and various outside activities.

The Superwoman Complex

You have probably seen a plaque, or paperweight, or bumper sticker with the message: "Women have to work twice as hard and be twice as good as men in order to get ahead. Fortunately, for us it isn't difficult." When I first saw that I chuckled and said, "That's true."

Well, as appealing as that may be to our feminine ears, it isn't true, because it *is* difficult. Often working women have double duties and responsibilities that pull them in opposite directions. To claim that it isn't difficult is misleading and inaccurate.

We have the added pressure these days of proving that women can handle jobs previously held by men only, and of never letting anyone think that we're less than totally capable. So, whether real or imagined, we often operate under the impression that we must be superwomen!

How Jesus Handled Fatigue

One thing I've always noticed about the Lord Jesus is that He never seemed to be in a hurry or frustrated, yet obviously He had to be tired and pressured at times. Just recently I was reading of the time when He was informed that John the Baptist had been beheaded, and He tried to get away for a few days of rest and mourning. But He could not get away from the crowd, even at that painful time in His ministry. The crowds always pursued Him, and He would give up His rest time to minister to their needs.

I read those passages and say to myself: "I want to be that way, too. I want to be able to give to others and not worry about my own personal needs. I want to be able to function under pressure and fatigue with the same selflessness that Jesus had. What keeps me from being able to do that?"

I began to analyze the kind of pressure I face and the kind of pressure the Lord faced. My problem, I realized, was not that I had too much to do, or that I was overcommitted. It's not possible to be overcommitted to Jesus Christ. And He was overcommitted to the ministry given Him, if you mean by that that every ounce of His life and energy was given to His ministry.

But Jesus kept a single focus in His life. Though He touched many people, gave of Himself continually, and had many demands on Him, He knew exactly what the goal was, what was important and what was not, and He kept *one* single purpose. He didn't try to be everything to everyone.

All Things to All People

What a relief it has been to me to realize that Jesus disappointed people at times. He did not always do what others thought He should do. In Mark 1:35–38, we read of one of these times, after Jesus had been up very late the night before, healing people at Capernaum:

> *And in the early morning, while it was still dark, He arose and went out and departed to a lonely place, and was praying there. And Simon and his companions hunted for Him; and they found Him, and said to Him, "Everyone is looking for You." And He said to them, "Let us go somewhere else to the towns nearby, in order that I may preach there also; for that is what I came out for."*

The disciples were urging Jesus to go back into Capernaum, where the crowds were waiting for Him. But Jesus, knowing exactly what His purpose was, chose to disappoint that crowd in order to do what He knew was more important.

That is a vital lesson for us to learn. It is not possible to be all things to all people. We must know what takes priority, and be willing to let other things go, even if it means disappointing someone.

Reducing the Number of Activities

One of my goals is to get the number of activities in my life reduced to a manageable level. I think many times my problem is not that I put in too many hours, but that my mind and thoughts are divided into so many different areas and activities, that I lack focus. And there's where the frustration sets in.

Now, how can we eliminate activities? I can hear some of you saying, "What can I leave off? There's nothing that's optional!"

Well, you might be surprised. The first thing is to sit down and make a list of everything that is on your slate to be done right now. Write every responsibility, every job, every involvement—in some detail. Maybe it's your job itself that is pressurized. Do the same thing with your duties on your job. Take the time to make the list, no matter how long it is.

Now, with the list in your hand, ask the Lord to give you wisdom about priorities. Then go down that list one by one and ask yourself this question about every item on the list:

1. What Would Happen If I Crossed This Job Off My List? You know what I discovered? Many of the things I thought had to be done, didn't! I could cross some items off that list and the world would not come to an end, my friends and family would not desert me, my boss would not fire me, and I would not be thrown in jail. It gave me some perspective.

You will be amazed as you go through your list that much of the pressure you feel is self-imposed. Even on your job, many of your "deadlines" are not set by your manager, but by you. Certainly there's nothing wrong with striving for excellence and being ambitious. But if you are pushing yourself so hard that you're fatigued and frustrated, you won't impress anyone very much. You'll start making mistakes and be difficult to get along with before you know it.

Now, once you've crossed off everything that does not have to be done, go through the list again, and ask this question:

2. What Can Be Postponed Until Later? Many things that you think have to be done today can easily be done later with no harm done.

I remember when I planned to wallpaper my daughter's room. We had chosen the paper, and I wanted to get started right away. But our schedule was truly hectic at that point. And I was getting all uptight about not getting her bedroom finished. She said to me, "Mom, I'm not putting any pressure on you to do that now. It can wait." She was a lot smarter than her mom that time. The pressure was self-imposed, and the job was easily postponed with no harm done.

Now, I'm not advocating procrastination. Many of us get ourselves into dilemmas by always putting things off. That may be part of the reason you're in that mess you're in now. When something has to be done, the best policy is do it now and do it right. That will save you more time and more headaches than anything else.

But if you've been putting yourself under pressure to get something done, and in reality there is no reason it has to be done immediately, postpone it.

Now, go through the list a third time, and ask this question about every item left on your list:

3. Who Could Do This Besides Me?　One of my biggest problems is that I try to do things that others could and would do, if I would just ask. I'm beginning to realize that I am very reluctant to ask people to do things for me. For some reason I feel guilty asking them to do something that I know I can do—especially if it appears that I'm trying to get rid of the dirty work. So, I keep heaping the details on myself to avoid feeling guilty, and then I'm exhausted, and I start to resent having to do everything myself. It gets to be a ridiculous cycle. And it's no one's fault but mine, because I haven't asked for any help.

Have you ever noticed that Jesus allowed His disciples to do a lot of the work? They took care of preparations, they took care of meals, they went out two by two healing and casting out demons, and telling others about Jesus. They were laborers together with Jesus, and Jesus didn't attempt to meet every demand personally. He shared His ministry with His disciples. We must learn to share with others, where we can.

Mothers, do you delegate responsibilities to your children as you should? Or do you still try to take care of too many of the details, things they could do for themselves? Maybe guilt feelings drive you to that, because you don't want them to suffer just because they have a working mom. Guilt is one of Satan's best tricks. Your kids are capable of doing a lot more than you think. Shed the guilt, and delegate some of those household chores. Your children will benefit from learning to be responsible, and they'll benefit from having a mom who isn't always tired.

I want you to know, as I keep telling myself, that nobody gives prizes for superwomen! Learn how to ask others to help you. Learn how to admit that you can't do everything all by yourself.

Now, after going through your list those three times, it should be somewhat shorter than when you started, and that alone should take some of the pressure off. The final question to ask is:

4. What Priority Does Each Item Remaining on the List Deserve? Stand back with objectivity and really assess which items are truly more important than others. And arrange your list in order of priority. Then plan a schedule—a reasonable schedule with realistic time frames—and start chipping away at the list, one by one. Don't think about the next item while you're trying to work on the first one. Keep your mind clear, focus on the task at hand. And do it now and do it right.

The First Priority

I've noticed when I get under pressure and time is short, that one of the first things I sacrifice is my personal time with the Lord. "After all," I rationalize, "the Lord understands my schedule."

For me, it is a constant battle to keep my time with God as my first priority. Unlike our jobs or other demands, there is no time clock to punch with the Lord. He does not issue us strict instructions on when and how long we should be with Him daily. He wants our heart's devotion, not a routine we go through to make us feel better.

Since our time with Him is just between us and God, and we are accountable to no one else, we begin to use that time as our "buffer." If anything has to give, our quiet time with the Lord gives.

It is no wonder that every Christian has to fight continually to keep a consistent, daily time with God. After all, our enemy knows how powerfully effective we could be if we spent significant time in prayer and meditation on God's Word every day. And Satan is a fantastic liar. Jesus told us Satan is a liar and the father of lies, and there is no truth in him (*see* John 8:44). If you are sincerely attempting to establish a consistent walk with God and a life of devotion, don't be surprised to find Satan very actively trying to defeat you. Here are some of the lies he tells us:

"You don't have any other option. If you take time for prayer today, you won't be able to get to work early, and that report will not be ready in time. It's not your fault. You have to do your work."

"You worked late last night. In fact, you've been working late a lot this week. You deserve and need a little extra sleep. God will understand."

"God doesn't expect you to pray and read the Bible

every day. After all, you are a working mother with two small children. You never have any time to yourself. You can only do so much. After the children get older, you'll be able to have a devotional life."

"You're just not a morning person. That's okay. It doesn't matter when you pray. Do it tonight when you get home."

"Hey, you don't have to do this every day. After all, you are not under the law anymore. Just do it when you feel like it. God doesn't want you to pray if you don't feel like it."

Undoubtedly, all of us could add lies to this list that Satan lays on us to keep us from spending time with God. The fact that he works so hard to prevent it should give us some idea of just how important it is in our lives.

As I read about Jesus, I see that the more pressure He was under, the more demands that were placed on Him, the more He got away and spent time alone in prayer. If Jesus needed that quantity and quality of time in prayer, how much more we do!

Overcoming Fatigue and Exhaustion

Here is a principle for overcoming fatigue and exhaustion that will work every time: *As the pressures, exhaustion, and fatigue increase, increase your quiet time with God in direct proportion.*

It is our natural tendency to do just the opposite. That's because we buy into Satan's lies. Resist Satan and his lies, and try this reverse principle. It is the example given us by our Lord, and *it cannot fail!*

Are you absolutely at the end of your rope? Then determine that you *will* spend a greatly increased amount of time
with God. Ignore your feelings. If you're exhausted, you
won't feel like doing anything except collapsing. Don't be
surprised that you don't *feel* like spending time with God.
Our feelings are not to be trusted. Remember this: *Feelings
have zero I.Q.* They are not intelligent. Sometimes they're
right, sometimes they're wrong. But you can never trust
them to accurately measure your spiritual temperature.

Don't be afraid to give up sleep time for prayer time. It's
no great sacrifice—it's a great privilege. I finally realized
that when I took away from prayer time to sleep, the sleep I
got did me no good. You won't suffer from spending time
with the Lord. Those quiet morning hours, before the world
starts to stir, alone with Jesus, will give you perspective and
peace and strength to face all the duties you have ahead of
you for that day.

There is nothing to compare with developing a personal,
one-on-one relationship with Jesus Christ. As I am writing
this, I think of my experience this very morning. As soon as
I got up, a worry started to take hold of my mind. I began to
think of what I should do to solve this particular problem.
Fear started to gnaw at my stomach. My head hurt. In a
matter of minutes, I was emotionally "fit to be tied," as we
say down South.

I did not want to pray. I did not want to sit still long
enough to pray or meditate. I wanted to do something about
this particular problem. But by sheer force of will, against
all my feelings, I pushed myself onto the sofa where I spend
time with God. (I find that it helps to have a special spot that
is your meeting place with the Lord.) I remembered that I

have to "bring every thought into captivity," and I began, slowly, to force my thoughts away from my concern, and toward God.

Gradually, the problem came into perspective. Through meditating on who God is, through singing some hymns which reminded me of His faithfulness and His protection, through expressing my concern to Him, through reading the Bible, through reciting many of His great and precious promises, my fears subsided, my concern was given over to His keeping, and my day then could begin with a light, free spirit. As a matter of fact, God showed me what a great blessing this particular situation could be in my life, because it offers me an opportunity to really trust Him in an area that is very new to me.

After time spent with God, my entire outlook had changed dramatically. Yes, it took discipline. No, I didn't feel like doing it. But I ask you, who benefited? Instead of facing my day with frustration, with a frantic outlook and with fear, I gained peace and assurance.

If a consistent time with God can give me that kind of outlook, can alleviate my fears, can calm my unrest, and give me direction, am I not then very foolish to let anything interfere with it? If time with God is the beginning of finding an answer to my pressures and fatigue, is it not a very poor economy on my part to eliminate that time in my schedule?

I am not a special case. It is no easier for me than for anyone else. I do not always succeed in applying this principle as I should. But I can testify that when I do apply it, it really works.

Remember the principle: *As the pressures, exhaustion, and fatigue increase, increase your prayer time in direct proportion.* I believe it is the essential foundational principle for a Christian who is battling pressure and fatigue.

Chapter Eleven

Working Mothers

You can usually spot working mothers. They have symptoms that are dead giveaways. They're frequently clock-watchers, waiting until a certain hour when they can call home to make sure that everyone is home who should be, leaving as soon as they possibly can to get home to their children and the other full-time job that awaits them when they get there. They rarely get to work early, because they are already up at the break of dawn just to get the kids ready and off on time.

Working mothers develop unique skills at telephone negotiation, as they settle arguments, dispense discipline, and issue instructions electronically. They frequently have worried looks, when they've left their child with a fever or an upset stomach, or when their four-year-old is not happy in the new day-care center.

Talk about fatigue and pressure! They're common symptoms among working mothers. They cook, wash, clean, chauffeur, tutor, and nourish one or more children between five o'clock and eleven o'clock in the evening, after working hard all day. When their children are between infancy and about ten years of age, they are usually more physically exhausted than anything else. Those are the years that the children demand a great deal of help with anything they do, from tying their shoes to homework assignments. Those are the years when children frequently do not sleep all night, and seem to get sick more often. Once the children reach the teen years, the *emotional* strain becomes exhausting, as mothers try to cope with the ups and downs of normal teenagers and preteens, while holding down a demanding job.

So, if it's so tough, why are so many mothers working? In November, 1984, the *New York Times* reported that 60 percent of all mothers work, including 46 percent of those with children younger than three and 52 percent of those with children younger than six. That means that millions of women leave home every day, dropping children at school or day-care centers, neighbors' or relatives' homes, and enter the working world. Why do they do it?

Some work because they really believe—or have bought this generation's philosophy—that a mother who stays home and does nothing but raise her children has little or no ambition or self-esteem, and is probably lazy. They believe they'll find the fulfillment that has evaded them as mothers, in a job or career.

Some work because they've allowed their standard of living to rise to such a level that luxuries now seem like necessities. They feel impelled to keep the family income at a high enough level that the family can have all the material things they've come to regard as necessary.

Some work because they truly love their jobs, and they love being moms as well, and seem to be for the most part capable of balancing the two roles.

But many—probably most—of these mothers have no choice; they are contributing support to the family that is necessary to make ends meet. Frequently they are the sole support of their families. If they didn't work, they would truly be without the basics of life—food, shelter, and clothing.

The Working-Mother Guilt Syndrome

I have some firsthand knowledge of what working moms go through, because I've been a career mom since my daughter, now finishing college, was eight years old. As I think back over the years, the one emotion that comes flooding back is guilt: Guilt because I was not home in the afternoon when Julie got home from school. Guilt because Julie didn't like the sitter very much, or because I could not go to her school during the day to be a grade mother, or take part in cookie sales. Guilt because the time I did have with her was occupied with housework, or work brought home from the office. Guilt when she became a latch-key kid in high school years, worrying about her feelings of loneliness. Guilt because she had to do more chores than most of her peers. The list could go on and on.

My whole upbringing and the role model I had in my very special and very traditional mother taught me, subconsciously, that mothers should live their lives for their children, should always be there for their children, should meet every possible need of their children—and anything less was second-best. I honestly cannot remember coming home from school when my mother was not right there, taking care of me and my brothers, cleaning, ironing, cooking, praying—and never wishing she was anything or anyone else.

So guilt was inevitable, as I struggled to be a good mom by the standards that I thought represented the best in mothering, and at the same time tried to keep up with a growing and demanding career. Obviously, it was not possible for me to be the kind of mom that I thought I should be, so I had to live with the belief that my daughter would have a second-rate mom. There seemed no alternative.

Undoubtedly, many working mothers reading this are experiencing this guilt I've described. And guilt that is not dealt with is a most debilitating, demoralizing emotion to live with. So, if you find yourself a guilt-ridden working mother, here are some suggestions on dealing with that guilt.

First, analyze the guilt that you feel. Describe it, at least to yourself, in detail. Write it down if you need to. But be certain that you know specifically what you feel guilty about. Do not allow that guilt to remain just a foggy feeling in the back of your mind. You will never deal with it until you spell it out in very clear words.

Once you do that, look at those guilts and answer this question: "Is it really right for me to feel guilty about this?" You need to be very objective, and perhaps someone else may be able to help you take that objective look. Pray about each of those areas of guilt, and ask for God's wisdom as you analyze that guilt. Come to a conclusion about whether or not this guilt is deserved.

Guilt can be either false or true—deserved or undeserved. But it feels the same either way, and we can be easily fooled about what kind it is. Just because you feel guilty doesn't

mean you are guilty. Guilt is one of Satan's best weapons—
false guilt, that is. And he uses it effectively to debilitate
many Christians.

True Guilt

True guilt is what we feel when God is convicting us of
some area in our lives that needs to be changed, and we are
resisting that change. God, however, never intends for us to
carry guilt around. He desires that we deal immediately
with any conviction that He brings to us, confess it, and
permit Him to change us. When we are convicted and refuse to take it to God for forgiveness and cleansing, that
conviction then turns into guilt. But that isn't from God;
rather it is a result of our failure to deal quickly and decisively with known areas of sin.

If you conclude your guilt is deserved, you will not have
any peace until you allow God to deal with it, confess it, and
change. For instance, if you are experiencing guilt because
you have taken a job which is so excessively demanding
that you are spending less and less time at home with your
children, perhaps God is trying to tell you that He wants
you home more often, even if that means changing jobs.

For a couple of years in my career I traveled extensively,
probably 35 to 40 percent of the time. My daughter was well
cared for, but for me to be away from her that much during
her early teens could not have been the best for her. I remember feeling lots of guilt as I rushed to an airport week
after week, made long-distance calls to see how she was
doing, and missed important days in her life. I rationalized
it away as necessary, but in truth it was not. There were

other jobs I could have held that would not have made those demands on me. But I didn't face that guilt; I submerged it and kept doing what I wanted to do.

That is not to say that all working mothers who travel should feel guilty about it. Each of us have differing circumstances. But if you are really willing to face the truth, you should be able to identify those deserved guilts that you are carrying around. When God reveals some of those areas to you, I encourage you not to hesitate in dealing with them. It may appear that the action required is too drastic, too costly. But nothing is more costly in the long term than for a Christian to refuse to deal with known areas of sin or disobedience.

False Guilt

It is my opinion, based on the working mothers I know, that a great part of the guilt these women experience is false guilt. For instance, if you are a single working mother, you're working because it is absolutely essential. The guilt you may feel because you go to work and leave a sick child with the sitter is probably not deserved guilt. The guilt you feel when you cannot be at every school function is another example of false guilt.

And all mothers have learned that kids are very good at laying on false guilt. I think children have inborn instincts for using guilt as a manipulative tool on their parents. Remember, just because your child tells you—either in words or in attitude—that you are the guilty party does not necessarily mean that they are right.

Furthermore, working mothers tend to do what divorced

parents do—assume that every problem their children have is a result of the fact that they have a working mom, or because their parents are divorced. That just is not the case. If you stayed home all the time and devoted every minute of your life to your children, they would still have problems that would baffle you. Just recently I had lunch with a wonderful young mom who has never worked. One of her four children is behaving in a most disturbing way. She is struggling with what is causing it and how to handle it. But the cause is not that she is a working mom, because she is not.

When you are carrying around false guilt, you need to deal with it just as quickly and decisively as you would true guilt. But of course, you deal with a different source when it is false guilt. Whether the false guilt is from Satan or from your own wrong thinking, it is certain that it is not from God. Therefore, to continue to carry that false guilt, once you recognize it for what it is, is both foolish and wrong.

Again, we need to pray much about it and ask God to deliver us. Then we have to watch our thought life. That is where false guilt begins, with our thoughts. And when that guilt is false, we are not allowed to think about it. Philippians 4:8 gives us our parameters for right thinking, and they are whatever is right, pure, lovely, of good report, excellent, and worthy of praise. False guilt is not right, it is wrong. Therefore, the guideline is clear: We should not allow ourselves to think those thoughts of false guilt.

The Apostle Paul told us that we must take every thought captive to the obedience of Christ (2 Corinthians 10:5). It won't happen unless we decide to take those thoughts and by an act of our will bring them into line with God's guidelines. In dealing with false guilt, we have to practice this principle over and over again, until we destroy that stronghold.

The minute those guilty thoughts start working on your mind, refuse to accept them and replace them with pure, lovely thoughts. If it only lasts five minutes, don't give up. Just replace them again. Depending on how long you've carried that false guilt, it may take a while to break that stronghold that it has on your thinking.

It is difficult enough to be a working mother without carrying around excess baggage. I encourage you to dump the guilt, whether it is true or false. Deal with it right away. The freedom and relief that comes as a result will give you a new lease on life. Your spirit will be lighter, your joy will be fuller, and your whole outlook on your situation will improve.

Deciding to Be a Mother

In the last few years, we've seen some real changes in women's attitudes toward motherhood. Only a few short years ago it was rare indeed for any young girl to even debate whether she would have children or not. Now, with people marrying much later and women pursuing new career opportunities, the decision not to have children is not at all unusual.

I am aware that some Christians believe that it is wrong for a wife or couple to make that decision. Frankly, I know of no biblical imperative that would require a wife to have children. Personally, I can see no problem with deciding not to have children, as long as both husband and wife agree.

However, I think the issue should be carefully and

prayerfully discussed before marriage. It is not fair to go into a marriage, leading your partner to believe you feel one way about children, and then later on inform him that you have strong feelings about children quite contrary to what he thought. I know couples where this has happened.

If you are thinking that you might not want children, investigate your feelings carefully. Be sure they are not simply selfish desires of preserving your freedom or your life-style. The Psalmist says that children are a gift from the Lord (Psalms 127:3), and any couple deciding not to have children should take that decision very seriously.

The Decision to Continue Working

A more common question faced by young wives is whether or not to have children and continue to work. I received a letter from a young wife, who told me that she wanted to have children soon. But her question to me was, "Is it right for me to have children when I know I'll have to keep working?" Many young wives face this question as they conclude that their second income will continue to be a necessity. And others face it as they realize that they do not want to give up their careers, but they want a family, too.

A Christian woman facing this question must have one overriding consideration, and that is "What does God want me to do about this matter?" God has the right to the final word in directing our lives, and since He is a great deal better at it than we are, you can trust Him implicitly.

Our job is to be willing to obey, even if it does not suit our plans or our ideas. We cannot come to God with preconceived ideas and plans and ask for His okay. We have to come with open hands and hearts and ask to know His plan and be willing to follow it.

It would be simple if there were a specific verse in the Bible that gives direct guidance on whether mothers should work outside their home or not. To my knowledge there is none. But this we know from Scripture: God is very concerned about the family. It is His basic building block for society, and family priorities are very high on His list.

With that in mind, let's look at this question of whether it is a good thing for a working woman to have children when she intends to continue working outside the home.

Starting a family is, as I've already said, a big decision, regardless of our circumstances. It takes a lot of thought and prayer. But I do not believe there is a right or wrong answer to this specific question.

There are many successful mothers who have worked even when their children were babies. And staying at home with your children is no guarantee that they are going to have a better foundation or be more secure and well-balanced than other children. I wish successful parenting could be reduced to a simple formula like "If mothers stay home with their children, they can be guaranteed that their children will grow into well-balanced, responsible, productive, delightful young adults." Parenting is the toughest job in the world, and there simply are no guarantees in parenting and no one parental role that works for every child. I don't think anything humbles you more than being a parent, for you realize very early that no matter how good you are or how hard you try, something can go wrong! It really keeps you on your knees.

However, the woman who is thinking of having children

and working at the same time needs to be well aware of what she is undertaking. Let me point out a few things that need to be considered.

1. In Order to Be the Mother You Want to Be, and Keep a Career Going, You Are the One Who Must Be Willing to Sacrifice. I think of my sister-in-law, who has worked almost continually while raising three children. It was not her first choice to continue working, but since it was necessary, she committed herself to being a first-class mother and maintaining her job as well. Her children are mostly grown now, and she and my brother have every right to be very proud of each of them. They are very special people, well-balanced, very secure, truly delightful young adults, all serving the Lord faithfully. But this did not come without a price to be paid—and the price was paid most heavily by the parents, and by mom, who had to give much more of herself and carry a more difficult schedule than she would have otherwise.

Now, if you asked her, she would tell you that she never sacrificed anything at all. She thoroughly enjoyed being a mother and raising her children. But certainly she had to give a lot more of herself as a dual-role mother, and she had to operate under more pressure and fatigue than she would have otherwise. But she made certain that her children never lacked the important things—time with their parents, lots of love and attention, and a sure knowledge that they were the most important things in her life.

Yes, it is possible to be a successful working mom. Absolutely. But before you commit yourself, make sure you understand the job you are undertaking. Read the "job description" very carefully. It requires extra sacrifice on your part, especially in those early years when the children demand so much attention.

2. A Second Consideration Is the Care of the Children While You Work.   With all the publicity these days about child abuse in day-care centers, I think working mothers and fathers have a very heavy responsibility to insure that their children's environment is not only safe, but conducive to their growth and maturity. I have to say that a child-care center would have to be exceptional for me to leave my young child there day in and day out. Our church operates an Early Childhood Center in Chicago, and in a center like this, you can rest secure that the care is very good and the environment is Christ-centered. But, of course, not every community has these Christian child-care centers.

When my daughter was small, I had a Christian friend who kept her in her home. That, of course, is a wonderful solution, if it is possible. As Julie got older and was in school, there was a retired Christian couple who came to our home and stayed with her in the afternoons and when I had to travel on business. That way her routine was not interrupted—and that was a real blessing. In the summers she spent several weeks with my parents in the South, and it was good to know she was under their love and influence for that time.

But, of course, not everyone has all these avenues open. You should, therefore, carefully consider how your child will be cared for while you work. It is a crucial decision, and if you are not convinced that you have a very suitable plan for that child's care, it should be a critical factor in deciding whether or not to have children and continue to work.

3. A Third Consideration Is to See if You Can Find a Way to Earn Needed Money Without Leaving Your Child.

Many women are very creative at doing this. Psychologists tell us that the first six years of a child's life are by far the most crucial. The love and care they receive in those years shapes their personality and character for the future. Therefore, being with them, especially during those formative years, is probably your best option. I know that is not always possible, but give it some serious thought. What could you do to earn money at home?

When Julie was little, before I was a single parent, I taught piano in my home. Later I cleaned our church to earn some extra money. That took one or two days a week, and I could take her with me. Now I know that is not an exciting career ladder, but it kept me with her during those early years.

I know women who take care of other children in their home, who sell cosmetics from their home, who do typing and bookkeeping at home. Many companies look for what is referred to as "cottage help"—people who will work for them in their homes, doing clerical, telephone, or other work.

Keep in mind that by working at home, you cut your expenses dramatically, so it isn't necessary to earn as much money. Without child-care costs—which are very high—*and* clothing and transportation costs, you could probably earn up to 50 percent less at home and still break even. Many times women just look at salaries and think the highest one is best. Don't forget those expenses. Sit down and figure it out. You may be surprised how much less you can earn if you can stay home and avoid those high expenses.

So, if you are a working woman considering starting your family and continuing to work, sit down and carefully count the cost. If you have the option to stay home during those early years, you would be well advised to do that, even if it means sacrificing a career opportunity or advancement. Remember, as a Christian mother, God will hold you responsible for the quality of mothering you give your children, but He really will not be much interested or impressed by how far up the career ladder you climb.

I know working mothers who could stay home but choose to work because they really don't enjoy the household routine. I understand that mind-set, because I've always felt that I would never be happy with *just* staying home. I am very active and need lots of things going to keep me from getting bored and lazy. But there are many things we can do while we stay home besides just changing diapers and washing dishes. Any creative woman can include things in her life that meet her own needs for self-improvement and advancement while remaining a stay-at-home mom.

For instance, get involved in a Crisis Pregnancy Center, or start a weekly Bible study for mothers, or a child evangelism class for the children in your neighborhood. Do volunteer hospital work, go back to school and finish your degree, go to evening classes to learn new skills, write a book. There are endless things we can do while we stay at home with our children that will give us the variety and the personal challenge and growth that are often lacking in the routine work of keeping house.

May I say, parenthetically, that if you think a job will relieve you of boredom and routine, think again. I have had lots of different kinds of jobs, from clerk to secretary to sales person to executive management to owning my own business, and *all* of them included routine, boring things that had to be done. Life is made up of a good number of routine duties, and the happy person is the one who learns to find meaning and joy in those routine things.

Priorities—Again!

It is so easy for us to focus on things that are not important to God. A working mother really has a balancing act to perform, and it is critical that she have a good understanding of what the priorities are. Many times, as working mothers facing day-by-day situations, we have to go back to the basics and remember our priorities.

I look back on my years as a working mother and sadly recognize that there were many times that my career took precedence over my role as mother. I really botched it badly at times. If I had it to do over, I'd do some things differently—probably turn down some jobs that I took and not worry so much about earning more money or buying a nicer home or proving to the world how successful I could be as a career woman. Is my daughter ruined? No, in His great mercy, God has covered for many of my errors and turned my ashes into beauty again. But undoubtedly Julie missed some mothering that she needed at times in her life. I cannot go back and fill in the missing blanks. God can do that for her, as she learns to trust Him, and He can use it for her good. I believe that strongly, and therefore I don't live in fear or guilt over my mistaken priorities. But both of us have missed some things we should have experienced because of my misplaced priorities at times.

Of course, every mother in the world will tell you that

you always wish you could go back and correct your mistakes. There's no way to do it perfectly as a parent. God does not need perfect parents, but He needs mothers and fathers who put Him first in their lives, and then put their families first in their priorities.

Let me reemphasize that parenting is a difficult task, though one of the most wonderful experiences in all of life. Being a successful mother does not depend on whether you work outside the home or not. I want to encourage the working mothers reading this, especially those who have no choice, that you can be the mother God wants you to be, and your children can have the attention and nurturing they need. You are not doomed for failure just because you work.

But there is a price to pay, and for working moms it is giving a lot of yourself, of your time and energy. Time that you might prefer to spend quietly reading, or time when you would like to go to bed early, or time when you really didn't want to go to a school function after working all day. These are the sacrifices that are very real for working moms.

The most important thing you can do is pour prayer time into this situation. A praying mom, one whose life is absolutely on track with the Lord, who spends time in His Word, and lives it before her children, is what your children need. You can be that kind of mom, whether you work outside your home or not.

I am aware that there are many different opinions on this subject, especially within the Christian community. I'm quite certain that many wonderful Christians would disagree with some of my opinions in this chapter on working moms. If you start asking advice, you'll probably get a different view from almost everyone you ask.

God's Leading

It is a great comfort to know that God does not lead us all exactly the same way. You need to know what God would have you do, and the marvelous thing is that He wants you to know that. If you will pray for His wisdom, and be willing to obey whatever it is, He will give His guidance to you personally. I am not the final word on this subject, and neither is any other person. But God is quite capable and most willing to impart His plan for you, if you are willing to listen and obey.

Back to basics again—spend much time getting to know God. Learn how to hear His voice and distinguish it from all others. That comes through time in His Word and in prayer, quality and quantity time. Keep that priority first, and you can be assured of His personal guidance for you as a working mother, or a potential working mother.

Chapter Twelve

Job Hunting
and Unemployment

L
ike most of you, I've gone through the job hunting routine more than once, with resumes and interviews and acceptances and rejections. Some of those job searches have been desperate, some have been more casual. Regardless, they all are exhausting, traumatic, and tense.

Job Hunting Under Pressure

Most people in the working world at one point or another begin to look around the job market to see if they can find a job they like better or one that pays more money. In fact, some people do it on a continual basis.

However, job hunting is a particularly difficult time when you're under pressure to find a new job, whether as a result of being laid off or fired, or entering the job market for the first time or reentering it after a period of absence. A pressurized job hunt can come about, too, when your current job is extremely disagreeable or the environment is particularly detrimental to your emotional, physical, or mental well-being.

It's that kind of pressurized job hunting that I want to address in this chapter. If you're not in that particular situation, I urge you to keep reading anyway. You never know when it may happen to you, and doing some thinking about it ahead of time is very helpful. All of us, too, know of people in this predicament, so we need to be aware of what they are experiencing in order to understand and encourage them.

Whether the pressure is financial, or from a desperate need to get out of the job you are currently in, the stress you feel is very real. Needless to say, that pressure very soon and very easily turns into anxiety, worry, and fear! These are the chief enemies of job hunters under pressure—worry and fear. If that's how you feel, then you're quite normal.

Let me ask you a question: Does it make any difference, at these times, that you're a Christian? It's so easy to quip a yes answer to that question, when things are going fine. But when you get up in the morning, under pressure to find a job, and there is that knot in your stomach, and you say to yourself: "What do I do today? I must find a job. What will happen if I don't find a job soon? Will anyone ever give me a chance?"—does it make any difference *then* that you are a Christian?

Recently I was discussing with a friend a really difficult situation she's encountering in her job. After we prayed together that God would make her victorious in this difficult spot, she said to me, "But it's so hard, it seems impossible." All of us can relate to that feeling. How many times have you thought and felt the same way?

Most of us, like children, long for easy ways out. And when it's not easy, we cry and complain. Those are normal human reactions. But Jesus came to give us the power to be abnormal! We don't have to be held captive by our normal human tendencies. Because of Jesus Christ, we can be absolutely joyful and peaceful in the midst of pressurized job hunting. That is victorious living, and if you're not experiencing it as a Christian, then Satan, your enemy, is robbing you of what is rightfully yours.

Why do you suppose that God is allowing you to go through this period of uncertainty and frustration? Why are you having to experience this seemingly debilitating and humiliating experience of being unemployed and looking for a job? If God is God, and if He really loves you as He says He does, why wouldn't He just land that perfect job in your lap and deliver you from all this torture? What possible good could come from this experience of job hunting under pressure? Consider some of these lessons:

Learning to Trust God

The most important thing to God is for us to learn how to trust Him. Could it be that this is the one sure way God could get your attention, and thereby teach you how to trust Him? If you can truly trust Him when you're out of work, at a time when you would normally be ravaged with anxiety and fear, when the future is unknown to you, then you know you're learning to trust. Could it be that you were looking to your job for security instead of to the Lord? Maybe He had to knock those props out from under you in order to make it possible for you to learn how to trust Him.

What I'm coming to understand is that it is at these really tough times that I have an opportunity to prove that Jesus Christ does make a difference in my life. Without these tight spots in our lives we would have no opportunity to find out experientially that God's promises are true and that He is truly capable of meeting all our needs.

I am in the midst of learning this lesson in my life now. Slowly I'm beginning to come to the place where I can truly thank God for tough, unpleasant, impossible situations—situations where my hands are tied, my options are gone, my efforts have failed, and my own ingenuity is ineffective. Gradually my earthbound mind is accepting the principle that it is only when everything looks hopeless and bleak that I can move into a new understanding of God and develop a deeper trust of Him.

When I truly can focus my mind on that truth, and when I can view my circumstances from an eternal perspective, then I can honestly say from my heart that I'm glad to have the opportunity to learn to know and trust my God in ways I never would have otherwise.

But I want to tell you that it is not easy, it is not once and for all. It takes discipline, a consistent devotional life, and a continual regrouping of my thoughts. When I say that I am just beginning to learn this, that is exactly what I mean. Learning is, after all, repetition. We learn to do things as we repeatedly try and fail, and try again.

Don't be discouraged when you find you must keep trying, keep starting all over again. Failure is not defeat. In this process of learning to be truly thankful for the unknown, uncontrollable, difficult circumstances of my life, I'm quite certain that my failures have exceeded my successes. But I just refuse to quit because down underneath all the fears and apprehensions that keep raising their ugly heads, I really do want to learn how to trust God in new ways. Sometimes I can even feel excited about the prospects, as I envision the joy and freedom of learning to trust God when there is no sight, there is no tangible reality, there is no human hope.

If it weren't hard, I could figure it out for myself, and just go merrily along. But when it is beyond me, when it is too hard for me, then I can have the great privilege of asking and allowing God to intervene, and watching Him change me and the situation. I am truly beginning to be excited about the possibilities of watching God work miracles, as I learn to trust Him.

Looking for Security

Have you been looking to your job for your security? Do you think of your job as your means of support? I have a Christian friend who used to work with me, and she would always say, "This company is not my source." I often think of Ruby, and remember that affirmation of faith which she taught me in a real way. No company can be my source of security or meet my needs. Depending upon a job, no matter how good that job is, is very dangerous ground.

When we can start looking to God as our security, and recognizing that we are His responsibility and we are not dependent on anyone but Him for our future and our security, then we begin to know real freedom. Ruby was laid off by that company we both worked for. It did not phase her. Not because she was independently wealthy, or was just working for the fun of it! No, she was not worried about being laid off because she had not placed her confidence in that job or that company, and being without that job was not a disaster to her. She simply expected God, who knew her needs, to give her something better.

Having recently started my own consulting firm, I no longer have that salary coming in every month. My income is not guaranteed. Of course, I have to spend time generating business, making presentations and proposals, and trying to convince other companies that they need my services. At this time as I write, I have an extremely important presentation for a prospective client coming up next week. I've prepared carefully for it, and I believe my proposal is a really good one for that organization. Securing this client is very important to my business, and most of my friends and family have been alerted to pray much for me during this period.

Now, I'm certain when I make that presentation next week, I'll have butterflies in my stomach. I'm sure I won't sleep too well the night before. But even with those predictable reactions, I can honestly say that I am not fearful about the outcome. God knows that I am His responsibility. He also knows a lot more about this potential client than I do. He may well see things that would be bad for me, that I could never see from the outside. Or He may want to test me further. Whatever the outcome, I feel very free and relaxed about this presentation, because God controls my future now, not me.

Trusting God really sets you free from worry about what's going to happen to you. That may sound terribly basic, but very few Christians ever get to that place in their walk with God. It is absolutely incredible how many of us continue to carry our own burdens and shoulder all the responsibility for ourselves. We won't allow God to be God in our lives, and to do for us what He is so totally capable and willing to do, because we just will not trust Him.

If indeed your current predicament of unemployment is the way you will learn to trust Jesus more fully than ever before, can't you agree that it is a good thing for you?

The Sin of Unbelief

Lately God has been showing me how He despises unbelief in my life. Not trusting God to do what He has promised is a very serious thing. It's not just that "we don't have enough faith." It is, rather, that we *refuse* to trust. That's what strikes me as I read the third chapter of Hebrews. The people of Israel *refused* to trust God, not because they didn't have enough faith, or they weren't spiritual enough or they didn't know enough about God. No, they *refused* to trust God because of the wickedness of their heart.

That's a pretty serious indictment, don't you agree? For me, the lack of trust in my life is taking on a new dimension. I no longer can excuse myself, or treat it lightly, for I'm beginning to realize that God doesn't treat it lightly. Not trusting Him indicates that there is wickedness in my heart.

And if I can indeed refuse to trust Him, then it means that I can do just the opposite also, and that is, make a decision *to* trust Him—or in other words, refuse *not* to trust Him. Trusting God does not depend upon my level of faith, or my stage of spiritual growth. It depends upon the set of my will, and no matter who you are or what your predicament is, you have the ability to decide to trust God. That is a choice you make.

If you're not yet trusting God in this situation of unemployment—or any other situation for that matter—will you just stop right now and realize that the reason you are not trusting is that there is within you an evil heart of unbelief. I don't mean to sound harsh, but I truly do believe that that is how God views our lack of trust. And if that is how He sees it, we really need to take this lack of trust more seriously than we have in the past.

Now, I want to encourage you that this is not a one-time thing. You must set your will to trust Him, and then determine that every time the doubts and fears come, you will by a set of your will, against all your emotions, stop and tell yourself and God that you choose to trust Him. Don't be stubborn like the people of Israel, who hardened their hearts and refused to trust God. But be willing to turn your will over to Him—many times.

Just this week a friend was telling me that she is very susceptible to a fear about whether or not she can perform her new job adequately. She knows that fear is of Satan, and she knows this is a satanic attack on her to try to destroy her confidence and her trust in God. She knows that through Christ she can overcome that fear. But even with that knowledge, she must continually remind herself, every time that fear raises its ugly head, that she has freedom from that fear through Christ. She has to stop and *again* set her will to trust God. Don't be surprised when this happens to you. It is true with all of us who are daily walking with the Lord as a life-style. Lessons God taught me in a dramatic way months or years ago I have to reapply almost daily. But each time I do, my faith is increased and my commitment is strengthened. And Satan's stronghold in my life is loosened each time I decide to trust God, rather than to give way to my fears and anxiety.

Becoming an Encourager

Perhaps God wants to teach you compassion so that you can be understanding and helpful to others who experience a similar difficulty. Second Corinthians 1:3–7 (YOUNG CHURCHES) says:

> Indeed, experience shows that the more we share Christ's suffering, the more we are able to give of His encouragement. This means that if we experience trouble we can pass on to you comfort and spiritual help; for if we ourselves have been comforted we know how to encourage you to endure patiently the same sort of troubles that we have ourselves endured. We are quite confident that if you have to suffer troubles as we have done, then, like us, you will find the comfort and encouragement of God.

If someone says to you, "You know, I was unemployed like you once, and I well remember how frightened and insecure I was," don't you tend to listen to that person with more credibility? They can really minister to you in your need. We need encouragers so very much in the body of Christ today. Maybe God is preparing you to be an encourager.

You can be sure that God has a purpose for taking you through this time of uncertainty and frustration. Now, can you be thankful that He is willing to take the time and effort

to shape you into who He wants you to be? Can you thank
Him for taking you through this experience so that you can
become more effective for Him? In James 1:2–9 (PHILLIPS)
we read:

> When all kinds of trials and temptations crowd into your
> lives . . . don't resent them as intruders, but welcome them as
> friends! Realise that they come to test your faith and to pro-
> duce in you the quality of endurance. But let the process go
> on until that endurance is fully developed, and you will find
> you have become men of mature character with the right sort
> of independence.

Can you truly welcome this period of unemployment and
this time of pressurized job hunting as a friend, rather than
an intruder? Will you believe that as a result you are going
to emerge from this experience with a steadfastness that
you did not have before, and that therefore you will be
more like Jesus Christ, and more usable in His service? If
that then is the case, isn't it worthwhile?

Let me, in closing, just remind you of some wonderful
passages of comfort and strength:

> . . . They who seek the Lord shall not be in want of any good
> thing.
>
> Psalms 34:10

> Don't worry over anything whatever; tell God every detail
> of your needs in earnest and thankful prayer, and the peace
> of God, which transcends human understanding, will keep
> constant guard over your hearts and minds as they rest in
> Christ Jesus (PHILLIPS).
>
> Philippians 4:6

My God shall supply all your needs according to His riches in Christ Jesus.

Philippians 4:19

Delight yourself in the Lord; And He will give you the desires of your heart.

Psalms 37:4

These promises are for you, if you are a child of God. You can claim them right in the middle of the unemployment you are experiencing. And you can prove in your life that they are really true.

Chapter Thirteen

Covering
Our Corner
of the World

Before He departed into heaven, Jesus told His disciples:

> *...You shall be my witnesses both in Jerusalem, and in all Judea and Samaria, and even to the remotest part of the earth.*
>
> *Acts 1:8*

Earlier we said that although we cannot preach or teach or continually witness, our lives can become that inescapable witness to what God can do for and with any person who is committed to Him. And we have talked a lot about how our behavior in handling many problems on the job can lead our colleagues to wonder and eventually to ask, what makes us different. But now let's consider witnessing in a more active sense.

What meaning does it have for us today to be witnesses in Jerusalem and Judea and Samaria? Well, when we look at a map, we see that Jesus was in Jerusalem, and Judea was the territory surrounding Jerusalem, and Samaria was farther away than Judea. So, Jesus is giving us a principle, that we witness first of all right where we are—whatever our Jerusalem is. And then we are responsible to let that witness grow and include the remotest parts of the earth.

Most Christians are willing to witness to the remote parts of the earth, by supporting missionaries, for example, but they won't tackle witnessing in their Jerusalem. That's truly getting the cart before the horse. Jesus said to start in our corner of the world, and for us working people, that has to include our jobs. It's a clear command from Jesus, and that elevates this issue to highest importance. Jesus said that if we love Him, we will keep His commandments, and He has commanded us to be witnesses right where we live and work.

Hindrances to Effective Witnessing

Recently a friend said to me, "You know, I don't really witness on my job. I know I should, but I don't. The problem is I have to go back the next day and face those people." I surely can relate to how she feels, can't you?

You know, I think the hardest place to be a witness is on our jobs, because we see these people every day. And they know us at our best and at our worst. When you're with someone on a day-in, day-out basis, you can't cover up. They know the real you. And I think one of the reasons we hesitate to witness is that we fear they will not accept our witness, since they know, and we know they know, that we're not perfect.

Furthermore, we tend to view our work environments as inappropriate places to witness. It's much easier to witness where the environment is conducive, and we don't feel very "spiritually minded" at work. Since spiritual subjects are rarely discussed in work environments, our doing so might categorize us as different, strange. And, let's face it, none of us wants to be rejected or unaccepted.

All of these feelings and others as well combine to make us tongue-tied and fearful of giving a clear-cut witness on our jobs. In fact, sad to say, there are many Christians whose co-workers would never guess that they are Christians. I know that has been true of me at times in my career.

Preliminaries to Effective Witnessing

Well, how can we overcome these hindrances, and become lights and witnesses in the part of the world to which we are sent? It begins with that changed attitude toward our jobs which we have spoken of. We cannot, consciously or subconsciously, see ourselves as "part-time Christians," fitting our commitment to Christ in around our jobs and other responsibilities. We cannot treat our jobs as separate parts of our lives—secular rather than sacred.

Second, in order to have a verbal witness that is effective in any situation, our lives must be clean before God. That doesn't mean we have to be perfect; it doesn't mean that because we've blown it at work before, no one will believe us. Satan tries to tell us that because we failed once, we're ruined. But that is a lie. God is in the business of turning our ashes to beauty, of taking our weaknesses and making us strong through them. You don't have to have an unblemished, perfect record in order to witness. But your life must be clean. If there is known sin, known rebellion of any kind on your part, your witness will be hindered. That's a basic principle we must understand.

Third, before verbal witness can be effective, there have to be listening ears. Jesus frequently said, "He that hath ears to hear, let him hear." That simply means that not everyone wants to hear, and without a desire to hear, a person will not hear. Of course, we don't know who those people are necessarily. But we must be careful not to verbally assault anyone with the Gospel until we sense an opening and a desire, no matter how small, to hear.

Jesus said, "Don't cast your pearls before swine" (Matthew 7:6). He certainly didn't mean that He considered people to be swine. It's just that we should not take something so precious and beautiful to us as our experience with the Lord and throw it in front of someone who has no sensitivity for the beauty of that pearl. Pigs have extremely poor eyesight, and can't distinguish things of great value.

To people in darkness, with poor eyesight, your pearl is indistinguishable from all the other garbage that is thrown in front of them. They get their kicks from drinking all night; you get yours from religion. That's frequently how they view it. And until there is some receptivity on their part, be careful not to throw pearls before swine.

I can think of a person in my life presently whom I want to witness to. I've made many attempts, but I can sense that the ears are not open. This person is just not the least interested in finding answers at this point. But I'm hanging in there, ready to talk when it's appropriate, saying whatever I can when I can, maintaining the friendship so that if there is ever an open heart, I'll be there, ready to witness.

I can also think of a particular occasion when I threw "pearls before swine." A past business associate and friend was in town, and wanted to get together for dinner. I remember that I had a most heavy schedule that week, and had reserved that evening to study and prepare for an upcoming speaking engagement. Yet, I felt it would be "selfish" of me to refuse the invitation, because I might have an opportunity to share Jesus with this friend.

As the evening wore on, it was impossible for me to turn the conversation to anything spiritual. My friend had a few drinks and was in no mood whatsoever to hear about my relationship with Jesus or what Jesus could do in her life. Instead, I had to listen to conversation about totally insignificant things, and when I did force a word or two of witness in edgewise, it was treated with disdain and condescension.

Though my motives were good, my discernment was poor. I had thrown my precious pearl before swine, and it just felt terrible. I wanted to yell, "Don't you understand, this is the most important thing in the whole world. Listen to me!" But I forgot that she had no way at this point of understanding the great value of my pearl.

When I finally got home, I said, "Lord, where did I fail? I wanted to share You with my friend. But it was just a terrible evening, and I wasted all that time, which puts me very much behind schedule now. What did I do wrong?" A couple of days later, as I was reading this passage in Matthew 7, God quietly explained it to me. I had a clear object lesson of what it means to throw pearls before swine. I discovered that I have to develop discernment for open ears, which are ready to hear.

Before people are going to treasure your pearl of knowledge about Jesus, there must be some awareness of its value. They must have some desire on their part to hear.

Creating a Desire to Hear

Now, think with me a minute: What does it take to create a desire to hear and know about God? What is the essential ingredient? It takes the Word of God—right? Romans 10:17 tells us that "faith comes from hearing, and hearing from the word of Christ." But how can we speak the Word to someone who has no desire to hear it? If it takes the Word of God to create a desire for someone to hear it, how do we get the Word of God to them in order to create the desire?

Did you know that there's more than one edition of the Word of God? The written Word of God, which we call the Scriptures, is not the only way to communicate God's Word. Listen to what Paul wrote in 2 Corinthians 3:2,3:

> You are our letter, written in our hearts, known and read by all men; being manifested that you are a letter of Christ, cared for by us, written not with ink, but with the Spirit of the living God, not on tablets of stone, but on tablets of human hearts.

This holds the key for us in discovering how we can witness. We have to be a living Word. When we live the Word of God before people, they cannot ignore it or dismiss it. And eventually when they *see* the Word of God in our lives, they're going to want to know more about it.

For instance, suppose you get to work next week, and discover that the place is in an uproar. Maybe you're a nurse, and every other nurse on your floor is angry at the head nurse. They're all griping and complaining, upset beyond words. Perhaps they even have a right to be upset. And, of course, they expect you to be upset with them, and to join in with their complaining and condemnation of the head nurse.

But suppose, without a word, you simply keep your cool, refuse to be drawn into the discontent, and remain peaceful and undisturbed. If you continue to abide in Christ in the midst of all that conflict, you've become a living Word. Your co-workers have just been forced to read the Word of God. They read Ephesians, or several Psalms, right there in front of their eyes. It came in a form they could not tune out or dismiss. And when the Word goes out it always accomplishes that to which it was sent. So that Word they saw in you began to take root.

If you consistently live the Word of God, eventually someone will be curious, and will ask you something like, "How can you be the way you are? How can you stay so cool in the midst of this dog-eat-dog environment?" They're asking you for answers!

Wow, this is what you've been waiting for. First Peter 3:15 tells us to always be ready to make a defense to everyone who asks us to give an account for the hope that is in us, yet with gentleness and reverence. Now, it's your responsibility to be ready for an answer. No faltering here, no hemming and hawing around, no hesitation. You have open ears before you, and now you give the verbal Word of God with clarity and love and gentleness. Now the value of your pearls is becoming clearer.

Each situation is different. We can say a lot to some people; others only allow us a few sentences here and there. But we must be looking for these opportunities to tell about the hope that is in us. While it's true that some Christians witness insensitively and do some harm in that way, it is far more often the case that we Christians don't use the opportunities we have. We are asked questions, in one form or another, that give us open doors, and we aren't prepared or willing to take our stand and give a strong witness.

Our Ultimate Role Model for Witnessing

Notice how Jesus witnessed to people. Sometimes He just dropped a statement that left everyone curious. People were always asking, "What manner of man is this?" There is example after example in Scripture of Jesus' method of witnessing, and it was always to create a desire and a curiosity on the part of the listener. Jesus asks the Samaritan woman for a drink of water. He didn't walk up to her and say, "Woman, I am the promised Messiah. Believe on me and be saved." What do you think she would have done if He had? Probably thought He was crazy, and gotten out of there as soon as possible.

Instead, He created a curiosity and desire in her to know who He was. He did not defend Himself against her charges. He ignored those accusing remarks she made. He kept looking for a way to make her want to know who He was. He continued to talk about living water. And then she said, "Sir, give me this water."

She asked Him for something. She didn't even fully understand it yet, but she wanted what He had.

That's our perfect model for witnessing. Create a desire by living the Word of God in front of your co-workers daily. If you display the fruits of the Spirit of God in your life consistently, you will be noticed. It will be different from what is expected, and you'll have opportunities to give an answer as to why you're different.

Missionaries to the Working World

If you, like me, have spent any time in an evangelical church, you have undoubtedly heard missionaries home on furlough testifying to what God is doing through them in their places of service. I can recall many stories of missionaries who spent years in a heathen land, tirelessly translating Scripture and learning the culture of those unreached people, waiting years for an opportunity to be able to clearly give them the Gospel. They tell how they became servants to these people, nursing them, teaching them, and building strong relationships with them in order to gain their confidence and earn their right to tell them God's Good News.

We hear those accounts, and our eyes fill with tears and our heart stirs within us as we thank God for their dedication, their patience, and their sacrificial love. And mentally, we put those missionaries in a special category of people (though they never want us to do that), and think of them as especially gifted and used of God to reach those poor dying souls who have never before heard the Gospel.

Are those souls in heathen lands more precious to God than the souls of the people with whom we work? No, of course not, because God is no respecter of persons (Acts 10:34). Well then, who is going to reach those people you work with? Does it not make sense that you have been put there as a witness, just as surely as the missionary was sent to unreached people?

If our avenue of reaching them is to create a desire on their part, as they watch our lives, then our lives are going to have to be quite different, quite unique. We will have to become servants, too, just as the missionaries do. Our serving will take different forms. Maybe it is helping someone else with a project and not receiving credit for it. Maybe it is enduring unfair treatment without complaining. Maybe it is refusing to defend ourselves when we are falsely accused, or purposing in our hearts to love people we don't like.

Whatever our particular circumstances, we cannot view our jobs as others view their jobs if indeed we want to be a missionary to that corner of the world. Instead of fighting for our rights, instead of complaining when the work is piled on, instead of looking for ways to cut corners, we look for ways to become servants, ways to let the love of God show through us. Because we know when that happens, we will create a desire on the part of others to know what makes us different, and then they'll start asking us questions, and we can do what we're really there to do—tell them God's Good News.

If missionaries are called to do that in lands across the sea, we are just as surely called to do that in our working worlds. If missionaries are responsible to witness to the people in their worlds, we are equally responsible to witness to those in ours. It is no easier for missionaries to become servants and give up their rights than it is for us. They are not given some special anointing that is denied to us. The power to do it is ours through the Holy Spirit. The command to do it is absolutely clear from our Savior.

When we stand before the judgment seat of Christ, shoulder to shoulder with missionaries and others who were in public ministries, do you really believe God is going to use a different yardstick for us than He does for them? If they are to die to themselves, so are we. If they are to sacrifice money, career, family, and so forth for the sake of the Gospel, so are we.

If we could just get this concept through to our hearts, and really change the way we view our jobs, we could win this world for Christ.

Isn't it apparent why God puts us in these environments with non-Christians? While most of those people might never read the Bible or hear it preached, with you there in the midst of them as an example of the living Word, they cannot avoid reading you. And that will create a hunger and thirst on the part of some of them.

Remember, Jesus taught us that many people will not receive the Word. He told us that the gate is straight and the road is narrow that leads to life, and few there be who find it. So don't be surprised when not everyone is interested. However, don't fail to give the Word whenever you can, even when it looks hopeless, because we can never tell what is in that heart, and what looks like tough, hard soil to us may be fertile, rich soil underneath. Our job is to plant the seed. We are not responsible for the outcome.

Using Failure as a Witness

I want to encourage you to set your mind toward becoming a witness. And I want to encourage you not to let past failure keep you from starting again. Don't let the fact that you haven't always been a perfect testimony keep you from becoming a witness for Him. None of us could ever be witnesses if that were true.

You know, you are not the only person in the world who fails. Isn't that good news! Learning to live and deal with failure is the subject of many books. Obviously, all of us deal with failure in our lives at some level or another. So, the fact that you have failed to be the "perfect Christian example" at all times is not an acceptable excuse for refusing to witness. I think many Christians fall into this "failure syndrome" and almost view it as real humility. Allowing past failure to keep us from witnessing is not an evidence of humility for a Christian. It is rather an evidence that there is lack of trust in God's power to forgive and restore.

Whatever your failures have been, if you've confessed them to God and received His forgiveness, you can still be a very effective witness for the Lord. In fact, God could even use your failures as a witness.

Let me give you an example. I remember one particular time when my behavior in front of one of my peers was anything but gentle, loving, kind, patient, long-suffering, or humble. Something had irritated me, and all those fruits of the Spirit of God that I should have been wearing just fell right off. (Undoubtedly it happened more than once, but this book isn't large enough to list all of them!)

I had been encouraging this colleague in things of the Lord, sharing my relationship with the Lord, helping him to begin a serious devotional life. And after all those "spiritual" discussions, here I behaved just the opposite.

When I got home that evening, God's Spirit really convicted me and I was truly embarrassed to realize how badly

I had blown it. My first thought was that my friend would now discount everything I had said before, that all that spiritual progress he had made would be lost because I failed so badly as a Christian, right before his eyes.

But the faithful Spirit of God showed me what I had to do. The next morning, as soon as I could, I got alone with my friend and apologized. I told him exactly how I felt, and how convicted I was, and how sorry I was that I had failed. But then I went on to explain how wonderful it is that even when we fail so miserably, God's forgiveness and His healing are always available.

Though I would have much preferred that the incident had never occurred, God in His great mercy and efficiency, used my failure to show this person another beautiful attribute of our Lord and Savior. He had an object lesson in front of his eyes of forgiveness. Our conversation revealed that failure and the fear of failure were real problems with this person. So, my failure became an avenue of witness to the wonderful forgiveness and acceptance Jesus offers to His disciples.

Just recently at my weekly small-group Bible study, one of the girls admitted that, without thinking, she had lied to her manager that morning. She was feeling very badly about it. We all could relate to her, because we all can remember times when we've done the same thing. "What do I do?" she asked. Our advice was to go right in the next morning, tell her boss exactly what had happened, apologize for the lie, and get it settled. And we pointed out how God could use even that failure—that sin—to speak to that boss. It could offer her a wonderful opportunity to explain why that lie bothered her so much, and why, though no harm was done, she could not allow it to be left that way.

Don't you imagine that her boss has lied before? Who knows, maybe she is right now struggling with a sense of failure and longing to know forgiveness and peace. Don't you imagine that her boss has had many employees lie to her before? But how many ever come back and admit it and ask for forgiveness? That failure can be used by God to bring a witness to His wonderful forgiveness that is available to everyone.

A Full-Time Commitment

I trust that you, as a Christian in the working world, have a proper perspective of your job, and that you view yourself as a Christian committed to full-time service to your Lord. He is worthy of every ounce we can ever give, and nothing else is of any eternal significance.

I hope and pray you have caught the vision of what could happen if every Christian in the working world became a "full-time" Christian, using his or her job primarily as an opportunity to share Christ in that corner of the world, in that Jerusalem. The potential is staggering. The command of our Lord is unequivocal and clear. The field is ripe unto harvest. And, oh, how our friends and associates in our business worlds need the message we can give them.